Beej's Guide to Network Programming

Using Internet Sockets

Brian "Beej Jorgensen" Hall

v3.1.2, Copyright © November 13, 2019

Contents

Intro

Hey! Socket programming got you down? Is this stuff just a little too difficult to figure out from the man pages? You want to do cool Internet programming, but you don't have time to wade through a gob of structs trying to figure out if you have to call bind() before you connect(), etc., etc.

Well, guess what! I've already done this nasty business, and I'm dying to share the information with everyone! You've come to the right place. This document should give the average competent C programmer the edge s/he needs to get a grip on this networking noise.

And check it out: I've finally caught up with the future (just in the nick of time, too!) and have updated the Guide for IPv6! Enjoy!

Audience

This document has been written as a tutorial, not a complete reference. It is probably at its best when read by individuals who are just starting out with socket programming and are looking for a foothold. It is certainly not the *complete and total* guide to sockets programming, by any means.

Hopefully, though, it'll be just enough for those man pages to start making sense... :-)

Platform and Compiler

The code contained within this document was compiled on a Linux PC using Gnu's gcc compiler. It should, however, build on just about any platform that uses gcc. Naturally, this doesn't apply if you're programming for Windows—see the section on Windows programming, below.

Official Homepage and Books For Sale

This official location of this document is:

- `https://beej.us/guide/bgnet/`

There you will also find example code and translations of the guide into various languages.

To buy nicely bound print copies (some call them "books"), visit:

- `https://beej.us/guide/url/bgbuy`

I'll appreciate the purchase because it helps sustain my document-writing lifestyle!

Note for Solaris/SunOS Programmers

When compiling for Solaris or SunOS, you need to specify some extra command-line switches for linking in the proper libraries. In order to do this, simply add "`-lnsl -lsocket -lresolv`" to the end of the compile command, like so:

```
$ cc -o server server.c -lnsl -lsocket -lresolv
```

If you still get errors, you could try further adding a `-lxnet` to the end of that command line. I don't know what that does, exactly, but some people seem to need it.

Another place that you might find problems is in the call to `setsockopt()`. The prototype differs from that on my Linux box, so instead of:

```
int yes=1;
```

enter this:

```
char yes='1';
```

As I don't have a Sun box, I haven't tested any of the above information—it's just what people have told me through email.

Note for Windows Programmers

At this point in the guide, historically, I've done a bit of bagging on Windows, simply due to the fact that I don't like it very much. But I should really be fair and tell you that Windows has a huge install base and is obviously a perfectly fine operating system.

They say absence makes the heart grow fonder, and in this case, I believe it to be true. (Or maybe it's age.) But what I can say is that after a decade-plus of not using Microsoft OSes for my personal work, I'm much happier! As such, I can sit back and safely say, "Sure, feel free to use Windows!" ...Ok yes, it does make me grit my teeth to say that.

So I still encourage you to try Linux[1], BSD[2], or some flavor of Unix, instead.

---

[1] https://www.linux.com/
[2] https://bsd.org/

But people like what they like, and you Windows folk will be pleased to know that this information is generally applicable to you guys, with a few minor changes, if any.

One cool thing you can do is install Cygwin[3], which is a collection of Unix tools for Windows. I've heard on the grapevine that doing so allows all these programs to compile unmodified.

Another thing that you should consider is the Windows Subsystem for Linux[4]. This basically allows you to install a Linux VM-ish thing on Windows 10. That will also definitely get you situated.

But some of you might want to do things the Pure Windows Way. That's very gutsy of you, and this is what you have to do: run out and get Unix immediately! No, no—I'm kidding. I'm supposed to be Windows-friendly(er) these days…

This is what you'll have to do (unless you install Cygwin!): first, ignore pretty much all of the system header files I mention in here. All you need to include is:

```
#include <winsock.h>
```

Wait! You also have to make a call to `WSAStartup()` before doing anything else with the sockets library. The code to do that looks something like this:

```
1   #include <winsock.h>
2
3   {
4       WSADATA wsaData;   // if this doesn't work
5       //WSAData wsaData; // then try this instead
6
7       // MAKEWORD(1,1) for Winsock 1.1, MAKEWORD(2,0) for Winsock 2.0:
8
9       if (WSAStartup(MAKEWORD(1,1), &wsaData) != 0) {
10          fprintf(stderr, "WSAStartup failed.\n");
11          exit(1);
12      }
```

You also have to tell your compiler to link in the Winsock library, usually called `wsock32.lib` or `winsock32.lib`, or `ws2_32.lib` for Winsock 2.0. Under VC++, this can be done through the `Project` menu, under `Settings....` Click the `Link` tab, and look for the box titled "Object/library modules". Add "wsock32.lib" (or whichever lib is your preference) to that list.

Or so I hear.

Finally, you need to call `WSACleanup()` when you're all through with the sockets library. See your online help for details.

---

[3]https://cygwin.com/
[4]https://docs.microsoft.com/en-us/windows/wsl/about

Once you do that, the rest of the examples in this tutorial should generally apply, with a few exceptions. For one thing, you can't use `close()` to close a socket—you need to use `closesocket()`, instead. Also, `select()` only works with socket descriptors, not file descriptors (like `0` for `stdin`).

There is also a socket class that you can use, `CSocket`. Check your compilers help pages for more information.

To get more information about Winsock, read the Winsock FAQ[5] and go from there.

Finally, I hear that Windows has no `fork()` system call which is, unfortunately, used in some of my examples. Maybe you have to link in a POSIX library or something to get it to work, or you can use `CreateProcess()` instead. `fork()` takes no arguments, and `CreateProcess()` takes about 48 billion arguments. If you're not up to that, the `CreateThread()` is a little easier to digest...unfortunately a discussion about multithreading is beyond the scope of this document. I can only talk about so much, you know!

Email Policy

I'm generally available to help out with email questions so feel free to write in, but I can't guarantee a response. I lead a pretty busy life and there are times when I just can't answer a question you have. When that's the case, I usually just delete the message. It's nothing personal; I just won't ever have the time to give the detailed answer you require.

As a rule, the more complex the question, the less likely I am to respond. If you can narrow down your question before mailing it and be sure to include any pertinent information (like platform, compiler, error messages you're getting, and anything else you think might help me troubleshoot), you're much more likely to get a response. For more pointers, read ESR's document, How To Ask Questions The Smart Way[6].

If you don't get a response, hack on it some more, try to find the answer, and if it's still elusive, then write me again with the information you've found and hopefully it will be enough for me to help out.

Now that I've badgered you about how to write and not write me, I'd just like to let you know that I *fully* appreciate all the praise the guide has received over the years. It's a real morale boost, and it gladdens me to hear that it is being used for good! :-) Thank you!

Mirroring

You are more than welcome to mirror this site, whether publicly or privately. If you publicly mirror the site and want me to link to it from the main page, drop me a line at `beej@beej.us`.

---

[5]https://tangentsoft.net/wskfaq/
[6]http://www.catb.org/~esr/faqs/smart-questions.html

Note for Translators

If you want to translate the guide into another language, write me at `beej@beej.us` and I'll link to your translation from the main page. Feel free to add your name and contact info to the translation.

This source markdown document uses UTF-8 encoding.

Please note the license restrictions in the Copyright, Distribution, and Legal section, below.

If you want me to host the translation, just ask. I'll also link to it if you want to host it; either way is fine.

Copyright, Distribution, and Legal

Contact `beej@beej.us` for more information.

Dedication

Thanks to everyone who has helped in the past and future with me getting this guide written. And thank you to all the people who produce the Free software and packages that I use to make the Guide: GNU, Linux, Slackware, vim, Python, Inkscape, pandoc, many others. And finally a big thank-you to the literally thousands of you who have written in with suggestions for improvements and words of encouragement.

I dedicate this guide to some of my biggest heroes and inpirators in the world of computers: Donald Knuth, Bruce Schneier, W. Richard Stevens, and The Woz, my Readership, and the entire Free and Open Source Software Community.

Publishing Information

This book is written in Markdown using the vim editor on an Arch Linux box loaded with GNU tools. The cover "art" and diagrams are produced with Inkscape. The Markdown is converted to HTML and LaTex/PDF by Python, Pandoc and XeLaTeX, using Liberation fonts. The toolchain is composed of 100% Free and Open Source Software.

What is a socket?

You hear talk of "sockets" all the time, and perhaps you are wondering just what they are exactly. Well, they're this: a way to speak to other programs using standard Unix file descriptors.

What?

Ok—you may have heard some Unix hacker state, "Jeez, *everything* in Unix is a file!" What that person may have been talking about is the fact that when Unix programs do any sort of I/O, they do it by reading or writing to a file descriptor. A file descriptor is simply an integer associated with an open file. But (and here's the catch), that file can be a network connection, a FIFO, a pipe, a terminal, a real on-the-disk file, or just about anything else. Everything in Unix *is* a file! So when you want to communicate with another program over the Internet you're gonna do it through a file descriptor, you'd better believe it.

"Where do I get this file descriptor for network communication, Mr. Smarty-Pants?" is probably the last question on your mind right now, but I'm going to answer it anyway: You make a call to the `socket()` system routine. It returns the socket descriptor, and you communicate through it using the specialized `send()` and `recv()` (`man send`, `man recv`) socket calls.

"But, hey!" you might be exclaiming right about now. "If it's a file descriptor, why in the name of Neptune can't I just use the normal `read()` and `write()` calls to communicate through the socket?" The short answer is, "You can!" The longer answer is, "You can, but `send()` and `recv()` offer much greater control over your data transmission."

What next? How about this: there are all kinds of sockets. There are DARPA Internet addresses (Internet Sockets), path names on a local node (Unix Sockets), CCITT X.25 addresses (X.25 Sockets that you can safely ignore), and probably many others depending on which Unix flavor you run. This document deals only with the first: Internet Sockets.

Two Types of Internet Sockets

What's this? There are two types of Internet sockets? Yes. Well, no. I'm lying. There are more, but I didn't want to scare you. I'm only going to talk about two types here. Except for this sentence, where I'm going to tell you that "Raw Sockets" are also very powerful and you should look them up.

All right, already. What are the two types? One is "Stream Sockets"; the other is "Datagram Sockets", which may hereafter be referred to as "SOCK_STREAM" and "SOCK_DGRAM", respectively. Datagram sockets are sometimes called "connectionless sockets". (Though they can be connect()'d if you really want. See connect(), below.)

Stream sockets are reliable two-way connected communication streams. If you output two items into the socket in the order "1, 2", they will arrive in the order "1, 2" at the opposite end. They will also be error-free. I'm so certain, in fact, they will be error-free, that I'm just going to put my fingers in my ears and chant *la la la la* if anyone tries to claim otherwise.

What uses stream sockets? Well, you may have heard of the telnet application, yes? It uses stream sockets. All the characters you type need to arrive in the same order you type them, right? Also, web browsers use the HTTP protocol which uses stream sockets to get pages. Indeed, if you telnet to a web site on port 80, and type "GET / HTTP/1.0" and hit RETURN twice, it'll dump the HTML back at you!

> If you don't have telnet installed and don't want to install it, or your telnet is being picky about connecting to clients, the guide comes with a telnet-like program called telnot[7]. This should work well for all the needs of the guide. (Note that telnet is actually a spec'd networking protocol[8], and telnot doesn't implement this protocol at all.)

How do stream sockets achieve this high level of data transmission quality? They use a protocol called "The Transmission Control Protocol", otherwise known as "TCP" (see RFC 793[9] for extremely detailed info on TCP). TCP makes sure your data arrives sequentially and error-free. You may have heard "TCP" before as the better half of "TCP/IP" where "IP" stands for "Internet Protocol" (see RFC 791[10]). IP deals primarily with Internet routing and is not generally responsible for data integrity.

Cool. What about Datagram sockets? Why are they called connectionless? What is the deal, here, anyway? Why are they unreliable? Well, here are some facts: if you send a datagram, it may arrive. It may arrive out of order. If it arrives, the data within the packet will be error-free.

Datagram sockets also use IP for routing, but they don't use TCP; they use the "User Data-

---

[7]https://beej.us/guide/bgnet/examples/telnot.c
[8]https://tools.ietf.org/html/rfc854
[9]https://tools.ietf.org/html/rfc793
[10]https://tools.ietf.org/html/rfc791

gram Protocol", or "UDP" (see RFC 768[11]).

Why are they connectionless? Well, basically, it's because you don't have to maintain an open connection as you do with stream sockets. You just build a packet, slap an IP header on it with destination information, and send it out. No connection needed. They are generally used either when a TCP stack is unavailable or when a few dropped packets here and there don't mean the end of the Universe. Sample applications: `tftp` (trivial file transfer protocol, a little brother to FTP), `dhcpcd` (a DHCP client), multiplayer games, streaming audio, video conferencing, etc.

"Wait a minute! `tftp` and `dhcpcd` are used to transfer binary applications from one host to another! Data can't be lost if you expect the application to work when it arrives! What kind of dark magic is this?"

Well, my human friend, `tftp` and similar programs have their own protocol on top of UDP. For example, the tftp protocol says that for each packet that gets sent, the recipient has to send back a packet that says, "I got it!" (an "ACK" packet). If the sender of the original packet gets no reply in, say, five seconds, he'll re-transmit the packet until he finally gets an ACK. This acknowledgment procedure is very important when implementing reliable `SOCK_DGRAM` applications.

For unreliable applications like games, audio, or video, you just ignore the dropped packets, or perhaps try to cleverly compensate for them. (Quake players will know the manifestation this effect by the technical term: *accursed lag*. The word "accursed", in this case, represents any extremely profane utterance.)

Why would you use an unreliable underlying protocol? Two reasons: speed and speed. It's way faster to fire-and-forget than it is to keep track of what has arrived safely and make sure it's in order and all that. If you're sending chat messages, TCP is great; if you're sending 40 positional updates per second of the players in the world, maybe it doesn't matter so much if one or two get dropped, and UDP is a good choice.

Low level Nonsense and Network Theory

Since I just mentioned layering of protocols, it's time to talk about how networks really work, and to show some examples of how `SOCK_DGRAM` packets are built. Practically, you can probably skip this section. It's good background, however.

Figure 1: Data Encapsulation.

---

[11]https://tools.ietf.org/html/rfc768

Hey, kids, it's time to learn about *Data Encapsulation*! This is very very important. It's so important that you might just learn about it if you take the networks course here at Chico State ; -). Basically, it says this: a packet is born, the packet is wrapped ("encapsulated") in a header (and rarely a footer) by the first protocol (say, the TFTP protocol), then the whole thing (TFTP header included) is encapsulated again by the next protocol (say, UDP), then again by the next (IP), then again by the final protocol on the hardware (physical) layer (say, Ethernet).

When another computer receives the packet, the hardware strips the Ethernet header, the kernel strips the IP and UDP headers, the TFTP program strips the TFTP header, and it finally has the data.

Now I can finally talk about the infamous *Layered Network Model* (aka "ISO/OSI"). This Network Model describes a system of network functionality that has many advantages over other models. For instance, you can write sockets programs that are exactly the same without caring how the data is physically transmitted (serial, thin Ethernet, AUI, whatever) because programs on lower levels deal with it for you. The actual network hardware and topology is transparent to the socket programmer.

Without any further ado, I'll present the layers of the full-blown model. Remember this for network class exams:

- Application
- Presentation
- Session
- Transport
- Network
- Data Link
- Physical

The Physical Layer is the hardware (serial, Ethernet, etc.). The Application Layer is just about as far from the physical layer as you can imagine—it's the place where users interact with the network.

Now, this model is so general you could probably use it as an automobile repair guide if you really wanted to. A layered model more consistent with Unix might be:

- Application Layer (*telnet, ftp, etc.*)
- Host-to-Host Transport Layer (*TCP, UDP*)
- Internet Layer (*IP and routing*)
- Network Access Layer (*Ethernet, wi-fi, or whatever*)

At this point in time, you can probably see how these layers correspond to the encapsulation of the original data.

See how much work there is in building a simple packet? Jeez! And you have to type in the packet headers yourself using "`cat`"! Just kidding. All you have to do for stream sockets is `send()` the data out. All you have to do for datagram sockets is encapsulate the packet in the method of your choosing and `sendto()` it out. The kernel builds the Transport Layer and Internet Layer on for you and the hardware does the Network Access Layer. Ah, modern technology.

So ends our brief foray into network theory. Oh yes, I forgot to tell you everything I wanted to say about routing: nothing! That's right, I'm not going to talk about it at all. The router strips the packet to the IP header, consults its routing table, *blah blah blah*. Check out the IP RFC[12] if you really really care. If you never learn about it, well, you'll live.

---

[12]https://tools.ietf.org/html/rfc791

IP Addresses, `structs`, and Data Munging

Here's the part of the game where we get to talk code for a change.

But first, let's discuss more non-code! Yay! First I want to talk about IP addresses and ports for just a tad so we have that sorted out. Then we'll talk about how the sockets API stores and manipulates IP addresses and other data.

IP Addresses, versions 4 and 6

In the good old days back when Ben Kenobi was still called Obi Wan Kenobi, there was a wonderful network routing system called The Internet Protocol Version 4, also called IPv4. It had addresses made up of four bytes (A.K.A. four "octets"), and was commonly written in "dots and numbers" form, like so: `192.0.2.111`.

You've probably seen it around.

In fact, as of this writing, virtually every site on the Internet uses IPv4.

Everyone, including Obi Wan, was happy. Things were great, until some naysayer by the name of Vint Cerf warned everyone that we were about to run out of IPv4 addresses!

(Besides warning everyone of the Coming IPv4 Apocalypse Of Doom And Gloom, Vint Cerf[13] is also well-known for being The Father Of The Internet. So I really am in no position to second-guess his judgment.)

Run out of addresses? How could this be? I mean, there are like billions of IP addresses in a 32-bit IPv4 address. Do we really have billions of computers out there?

Yes.

Also, in the beginning, when there were only a few computers and everyone thought a billion was an impossibly large number, some big organizations were generously allocated

---

[13]https://en.wikipedia.org/wiki/Vint_Cerf

millions of IP addresses for their own use. (Such as Xerox, MIT, Ford, HP, IBM, GE, AT&T, and some little company called Apple, to name a few.)

In fact, if it weren't for several stopgap measures, we would have run out a long time ago.

But now we're living in an era where we're talking about every human having an IP address, every computer, every calculator, every phone, every parking meter, and (why not) every puppy dog, as well.

And so, IPv6 was born. Since Vint Cerf is probably immortal (even if his physical form should pass on, heaven forbid, he is probably already existing as some kind of hyper-intelligent ELIZA[14] program out in the depths of the Internet2), no one wants to have to hear him say again "I told you so" if we don't have enough addresses in the next version of the Internet Protocol.

What does this suggest to you?

That we need a *lot* more addresses. That we need not just twice as many addresses, not a billion times as many, not a thousand trillion times as many, but *79 MILLION BILLION TRILLION times as many possible addresses!* That'll show 'em!

You're saying, "Beej, is that true? I have every reason to disbelieve large numbers." Well, the difference between 32 bits and 128 bits might not sound like a lot; it's only 96 more bits, right? But remember, we're talking powers here: 32 bits represents some 4 billion numbers (2^{32}), while 128 bits represents about 340 trillion trillion trillion numbers (for real, 2^{128}). That's like a million IPv4 Internets for *every single star in the Universe*.

Forget this dots-and-numbers look of IPv4, too; now we've got a hexadecimal representation, with each two-byte chunk separated by a colon, like this:

```
2001:0db8:c9d2:aee5:73e3:934a:a5ae:9551
```

That's not all! Lots of times, you'll have an IP address with lots of zeros in it, and you can compress them between two colons. And you can leave off leading zeros for each byte pair. For instance, each of these pairs of addresses are equivalent:

```
2001:0db8:c9d2:0012:0000:0000:0000:0051
2001:db8:c9d2:12::51

2001:0db8:ab00:0000:0000:0000:0000:0000
2001:db8:ab00::

0000:0000:0000:0000:0000:0000:0000:0001
::1
```

The address `::1` is the *loopback address*. It always means "this machine I'm running on now". In IPv4, the loopback address is `127.0.0.1`.

---

[14]https://en.wikipedia.org/wiki/ELIZA

Finally, there's an IPv4-compatibility mode for IPv6 addresses that you might come across. If you want, for example, to represent the IPv4 address 192.0.2.33 as an IPv6 address, you use the following notation: ":::ffff:192.0.2.33".

We're talking serious fun.

In fact, it's such serious fun, that the Creators of IPv6 have quite cavalierly lopped off trillions and trillions of addresses for reserved use, but we have so many, frankly, who's even counting anymore? There are plenty left over for every man, woman, child, puppy, and parking meter on every planet in the galaxy. And believe me, every planet in the galaxy has parking meters. You know it's true.

Subnets

For organizational reasons, it's sometimes convenient to declare that "this first part of this IP address up through this bit is the *network portion* of the IP address, and the remainder is the *host portion*.

For instance, with IPv4, you might have 192.0.2.12, and we could say that the first three bytes are the network and the last byte was the host. Or, put another way, we're talking about host 12 on network 192.0.2.0 (see how we zero out the byte that was the host).

And now for more outdated information! Ready? In the Ancient Times, there were "classes" of subnets, where the first one, two, or three bytes of the address was the network part. If you were lucky enough to have one byte for the network and three for the host, you could have 24 bits-worth of hosts on your network (16 million or so). That was a "Class A" network. On the opposite end was a "Class C", with three bytes of network, and one byte of host (256 hosts, minus a couple that were reserved).

So as you can see, there were just a few Class As, a huge pile of Class Cs, and some Class Bs in the middle.

The network portion of the IP address is described by something called the *netmask*, which you bitwise-AND with the IP address to get the network number out of it. The netmask usually looks something like 255.255.255.0. (E.g. with that netmask, if your IP is 192.0.2.12, then your network is 192.0.2.12 AND 255.255.255.0 which gives 192.0.2.0.)

Unfortunately, it turned out that this wasn't fine-grained enough for the eventual needs of the Internet; we were running out of Class C networks quite quickly, and we were most definitely out of Class As, so don't even bother to ask. To remedy this, The Powers That Be allowed for the netmask to be an arbitrary number of bits, not just 8, 16, or 24. So you might have a netmask of, say 255.255.255.252, which is 30 bits of network, and 2 bits of host allowing for four hosts on the network. (Note that the netmask is *ALWAYS* a bunch of 1-bits followed by a bunch of 0-bits.)

But it's a bit unwieldy to use a big string of numbers like 255.192.0.0 as a netmask. First of all, people don't have an intuitive idea of how many bits that is, and secondly, it's really not compact. So the New Style came along, and it's much nicer. You just put a slash after the IP address, and then follow that by the number of network bits in decimal. Like this: `192.0.2.12/30`.

Or, for IPv6, something like this: `2001:db8::/32` or `2001:db8:5413:4028::9db9/64`.

Port Numbers

If you'll kindly remember, I presented you earlier with the Layered Network Model which had the Internet Layer (IP) split off from the Host-to-Host Transport Layer (TCP and UDP). Get up to speed on that before the next paragraph.

Turns out that besides an IP address (used by the IP layer), there is another address that is used by TCP (stream sockets) and, coincidentally, by UDP (datagram sockets). It is the *port number*. It's a 16-bit number that's like the local address for the connection.

Think of the IP address as the street address of a hotel, and the port number as the room number. That's a decent analogy; maybe later I'll come up with one involving the automobile industry.

Say you want to have a computer that handles incoming mail AND web services—how do you differentiate between the two on a computer with a single IP address?

Well, different services on the Internet have different well-known port numbers. You can see them all in the Big IANA Port List[15] or, if you're on a Unix box, in your `/etc/services` file. HTTP (the web) is port 80, telnet is port 23, SMTP is port 25, the game DOOM[16] used port 666, etc. and so on. Ports under 1024 are often considered special, and usually require special OS privileges to use.

And that's about it!

Byte Order

By Order of the Realm! There shall be two byte orderings, hereafter to be known as Lame and Magnificent!

I joke, but one really is better than the other. :-)

There really is no easy way to say this, so I'll just blurt it out: your computer might have been storing bytes in reverse order behind your back. I know! No one wanted to have to tell you.

The thing is, everyone in the Internet world has generally agreed that if you want to represent the two-byte hex number, say `b34f`, you'll store it in two sequential bytes `b3` followed by

---

[15]https://www.iana.org/assignments/port-numbers
[16]https://en.wikipedia.org/wiki/Doom_(1993_video_game)

4f. Makes sense, and, as Wilford Brimley[17] would tell you, it's the Right Thing To Do. This number, stored with the big end first, is called *Big-Endian*.

Unfortunately, a *few* computers scattered here and there throughout the world, namely anything with an Intel or Intel-compatible processor, store the bytes reversed, so b34f would be stored in memory as the sequential bytes 4f followed by b3. This storage method is called *Little-Endian*.

But wait, I'm not done with terminology yet! The more-sane *Big-Endian* is also called *Network Byte Order* because that's the order us network types like.

Your computer stores numbers in *Host Byte Order*. If it's an Intel 80x86, Host Byte Order is Little-Endian. If it's a Motorola 68k, Host Byte Order is Big-Endian. If it's a PowerPC, Host Byte Order is… well, it depends!

A lot of times when you're building packets or filling out data structures you'll need to make sure your two- and four-byte numbers are in Network Byte Order. But how can you do this if you don't know the native Host Byte Order?

Good news! You just get to assume the Host Byte Order isn't right, and you always run the value through a function to set it to Network Byte Order. The function will do the magic conversion if it has to, and this way your code is portable to machines of differing endianness.

All righty. There are two types of numbers that you can convert: short (two bytes) and long (four bytes). These functions work for the unsigned variations as well. Say you want to convert a short from Host Byte Order to Network Byte Order. Start with "h" for "host", follow it with "to", then "n" for "network", and "s" for "short": h-to-n-s, or htons() (read: "Host to Network Short").

It's almost too easy…

You can use every combination of "n", "h", "s", and "l" you want, not counting the really stupid ones. For example, there is NOT a stolh() ("Short to Long Host") function—not at this party, anyway. But there are:

Function	Description
htons()	host to network short
htonl()	host to network long
ntohs()	network to host short
ntohl()	network to host long

Basically, you'll want to convert the numbers to Network Byte Order before they go out on the wire, and convert them to Host Byte Order as they come in off the wire.

---

[17] https://en.wikipedia.org/wiki/Wilford_Brimley

I don't know of a 64-bit variant, sorry. And if you want to do floating point, check out the section on Serialization, far below.

Assume the numbers in this document are in Host Byte Order unless I say otherwise.

structs

Well, we're finally here. It's time to talk about programming. In this section, I'll cover various data types used by the sockets interface, since some of them are a real bear to figure out.

First the easy one: a socket descriptor. A socket descriptor is the following type:

```
int
```

Just a regular `int`.

Things get weird from here, so just read through and bear with me.

My First Struct™—`struct addrinfo`. This structure is a more recent invention, and is used to prep the socket address structures for subsequent use. It's also used in host name lookups, and service name lookups. That'll make more sense later when we get to actual usage, but just know for now that it's one of the first things you'll call when making a connection.

```
struct addrinfo {
    int              ai_flags;      // AI_PASSIVE, AI_CANONNAME, etc.
    int              ai_family;     // AF_INET, AF_INET6, AF_UNSPEC
    int              ai_socktype;   // SOCK_STREAM, SOCK_DGRAM
    int              ai_protocol;   // use 0 for "any"
    size_t           ai_addrlen;    // size of ai_addr in bytes
    struct sockaddr *ai_addr;       // struct sockaddr_in or _in6
    char            *ai_canonname;  // full canonical hostname

    struct addrinfo *ai_next;       // linked list, next node
};
```

You'll load this struct up a bit, and then call `getaddrinfo()`. It'll return a pointer to a new linked list of these structures filled out with all the goodies you need.

You can force it to use IPv4 or IPv6 in the `ai_family` field, or leave it as `AF_UNSPEC` to use whatever. This is cool because your code can be IP version-agnostic.

Note that this is a linked list: `ai_next` points at the next element—there could be several results for you to choose from. I'd use the first result that worked, but you might have different business needs; I don't know everything, man!

You'll see that the `ai_addr` field in the `struct addrinfo` is a pointer to a `struct sockaddr`. This is where we start getting into the nitty-gritty details of what's inside an IP address structure.

You might not usually need to write to these structures; oftentimes, a call to `getaddrinfo()` to fill out your `struct addrinfo` for you is all you'll need. You *will*, however, have to peer inside these `struct`s to get the values out, so I'm presenting them here.

(Also, all the code written before `struct addrinfo` was invented we packed all this stuff by hand, so you'll see a lot of IPv4 code out in the wild that does exactly that. You know, in old versions of this guide and so on.)

Some `struct`s are IPv4, some are IPv6, and some are both. I'll make notes of which are what.

Anyway, the `struct sockaddr` holds socket address information for many types of sockets.

```
struct sockaddr {
    unsigned short    sa_family;    // address family, AF_xxx
    char              sa_data[14];  // 14 bytes of protocol address
};
```

`sa_family` can be a variety of things, but it'll be AF_INET (IPv4) or AF_INET6 (IPv6) for everything we do in this document. `sa_data` contains a destination address and port number for the socket. This is rather unwieldy since you don't want to tediously pack the address in the `sa_data` by hand.

To deal with `struct sockaddr`, programmers created a parallel structure: `struct sockaddr_in` ("in" for "Internet") to be used with IPv4.

And *this is the important* bit: a pointer to a `struct sockaddr_in` can be cast to a pointer to a `struct sockaddr` and vice-versa. So even though `connect()` wants a `struct sockaddr*`, you can still use a `struct sockaddr_in` and cast it at the last minute!

```
// (IPv4 only--see struct sockaddr_in6 for IPv6)

struct sockaddr_in {
    short int          sin_family;  // Address family, AF_INET
    unsigned short int sin_port;    // Port number
    struct in_addr     sin_addr;    // Internet address
    unsigned char      sin_zero[8]; // Same size as struct sockaddr
};
```

This structure makes it easy to reference elements of the socket address. Note that `sin_zero` (which is included to pad the structure to the length of a `struct sockaddr`) should be set to all zeros with the function `memset()`. Also, notice that `sin_family` corresponds to sa_family in a struct sockaddr and should be set to "AF_INET". Finally, the sin_port must be in *Network Byte Order* (by using htons()!)

Let's dig deeper! You see the sin_addr field is a struct in_addr. What is that thing? Well, not to be overly dramatic, but it's one of the scariest unions of all time:

```
// (IPv4 only--see struct in6_addr for IPv6)

// Internet address (a structure for historical reasons)
struct in_addr {
    uint32_t s_addr; // that's a 32-bit int (4 bytes)
};
```

Whoa! Well, it *used* to be a union, but now those days seem to be gone. Good riddance. So if you have declared ina to be of type struct sockaddr_in, then ina.sin_addr.s_addr references the 4-byte IP address (in Network Byte Order). Note that even if your system still uses the God-awful union for struct in_addr, you can still reference the 4-byte IP address in exactly the same way as I did above (this due to #defines).

What about IPv6? Similar structs exist for it, as well:

```
// (IPv6 only--see struct sockaddr_in and struct in_addr for IPv4)

struct sockaddr_in6 {
    u_int16_t      sin6_family;   // address family, AF_INET6
    u_int16_t      sin6_port;     // port number, Network Byte Order
    u_int32_t      sin6_flowinfo; // IPv6 flow information
    struct in6_addr sin6_addr;    // IPv6 address
    u_int32_t      sin6_scope_id; // Scope ID
};

struct in6_addr {
    unsigned char  s6_addr[16];   // IPv6 address
};
```

Note that IPv6 has an IPv6 address and a port number, just like IPv4 has an IPv4 address and a port number.

Also note that I'm not going to talk about the IPv6 flow information or Scope ID fields for the moment... this is just a starter guide. :-)

Last but not least, here is another simple structure, struct sockaddr_storage that is designed to be large enough to hold both IPv4 and IPv6 structures. See, for some calls, sometimes you don't know in advance if it's going to fill out your struct sockaddr with an IPv4 or IPv6 address. So you pass in this parallel structure, very similar to struct sockaddr except larger, and then cast it to the type you need:

```
struct sockaddr_storage {
    sa_family_t  ss_family;      // address family

    // all this is padding, implementation specific, ignore it:
    char      __ss_pad1[_SS_PAD1SIZE];
    int64_t   __ss_align;
    char      __ss_pad2[_SS_PAD2SIZE];
};
```

What's important is that you can see the address family in the `ss_family` field—check this to see if it's `AF_INET` or `AF_INET6` (for IPv4 or IPv6). Then you can cast it to a `struct sockaddr_in` or `struct sockaddr_in6` if you wanna.

IP Addresses, Part Deux

Fortunately for you, there are a bunch of functions that allow you to manipulate IP addresses. No need to figure them out by hand and stuff them in a `long` with the `<<` operator.

First, let's say you have a `struct sockaddr_in ina`, and you have an IP address "10.12.110.57" or "2001:db8:63b3:1::3490" that you want to store into it. The function you want to use, `inet_pton()`, converts an IP address in numbers-and-dots notation into either a `struct in_addr` or a `struct in6_addr` depending on whether you specify `AF_INET` or `AF_INET6`. ("pton" stands for "presentation to network"—you can call it "printable to network" if that's easier to remember.) The conversion can be made as follows:

```
struct sockaddr_in sa; // IPv4
struct sockaddr_in6 sa6; // IPv6

inet_pton(AF_INET, "10.12.110.57", &(sa.sin_addr)); // IPv4
inet_pton(AF_INET6, "2001:db8:63b3:1::3490", &(sa6.sin6_addr)); // IPv6
```

(Quick note: the old way of doing things used a function called `inet_addr()` or another function called `inet_aton()`; these are now obsolete and don't work with IPv6.)

Now, the above code snippet isn't very robust because there is no error checking. See, `inet_pton()` returns -1 on error, or 0 if the address is messed up. So check to make sure the result is greater than 0 before using!

All right, now you can convert string IP addresses to their binary representations. What about the other way around? What if you have a `struct in_addr` and you want to print it in numbers-and-dots notation? (Or a `struct in6_addr` that you want in, uh, "hex-and-colons" notation.) In this case, you'll want to use the function `inet_ntop()` ("ntop" means "network to presentation"—you can call it "network to printable" if that's easier to remember), like this:

```
1   // IPv4:
2
3   char ip4[INET_ADDRSTRLEN];   // space to hold the IPv4 string
4   struct sockaddr_in sa;       // pretend this is loaded with something
5
6   inet_ntop(AF_INET, &(sa.sin_addr), ip4, INET_ADDRSTRLEN);
7
8   printf("The IPv4 address is: %s\n", ip4);
9
10
11  // IPv6:
12
13  char ip6[INET6_ADDRSTRLEN]; // space to hold the IPv6 string
14  struct sockaddr_in6 sa6;     // pretend this is loaded with something
15
16  inet_ntop(AF_INET6, &(sa6.sin6_addr), ip6, INET6_ADDRSTRLEN);
17
18  printf("The address is: %s\n", ip6);
```

When you call it, you'll pass the address type (IPv4 or IPv6), the address, a pointer to a string to hold the result, and the maximum length of that string. (Two macros conveniently hold the size of the string you'll need to hold the largest IPv4 or IPv6 address: INET_ADDRSTRLEN and INET6_ADDRSTRLEN.)

(Another quick note to mention once again the old way of doing things: the historical function to do this conversion was called inet_ntoa(). It's also obsolete and won't work with IPv6.)

Lastly, these functions only work with numeric IP addresses—they won't do any nameserver DNS lookup on a hostname, like "www.example.com". You will use getaddrinfo() to do that, as you'll see later on.

Private (Or Disconnected) Networks

Lots of places have a firewall that hides the network from the rest of the world for their own protection. And often times, the firewall translates "internal" IP addresses to "external" (that everyone else in the world knows) IP addresses using a process called *Network Address Translation*, or NAT.

Are you getting nervous yet? "Where's he going with all this weird stuff?"

Well, relax and buy yourself a non-alcoholic (or alcoholic) drink, because as a beginner, you don't even have to worry about NAT, since it's done for you transparently. But I wanted to talk about the network behind the firewall in case you started getting confused by the network numbers you were seeing.

For instance, I have a firewall at home. I have two static IPv4 addresses allocated to me by the DSL company, and yet I have seven computers on the network. How is this possible? Two computers can't share the same IP address, or else the data wouldn't know which one to go to!

The answer is: they don't share the same IP addresses. They are on a private network with 24 million IP addresses allocated to it. They are all just for me. Well, all for me as far as anyone else is concerned. Here's what's happening:

If I log into a remote computer, it tells me I'm logged in from 192.0.2.33 which is the public IP address my ISP has provided to me. But if I ask my local computer what its IP address is, it says 10.0.0.5. Who is translating the IP address from one to the other? That's right, the firewall! It's doing NAT!

`10.x.x.x` is one of a few reserved networks that are only to be used either on fully disconnected networks, or on networks that are behind firewalls. The details of which private network numbers are available for you to use are outlined in RFC 1918[18], but some common ones you'll see are `10.x.x.x` and `192.168.x.x`, where x is 0-255, generally. Less common is `172.y.x.x`, where y goes between 16 and 31.

Networks behind a NATing firewall don't *need* to be on one of these reserved networks, but they commonly are.

(Fun fact! My external IP address isn't really `192.0.2.33`. The `192.0.2.x` network is reserved for make-believe "real" IP addresses to be used in documentation, just like this guide! Wowzers!)

IPv6 has private networks, too, in a sense. They'll start with `fdXX:` (or maybe in the future `fcXX:`), as per RFC 4193[19]. NAT and IPv6 don't generally mix, however (unless you're doing the IPv6 to IPv4 gateway thing which is beyond the scope of this document)—in theory you'll have so many addresses at your disposal that you won't need to use NAT any longer. But if you want to allocate addresses for yourself on a network that won't route outside, this is how to do it.

---

[18]https://tools.ietf.org/html/rfc1918
[19]https://tools.ietf.org/html/rfc4193

Jumping from IPv4 to IPv6

But I just want to know what to change in my code to get it going with IPv6! Tell me now!

Ok! Ok!

Almost everything in here is something I've gone over, above, but it's the short version for the impatient. (Of course, there is more than this, but this is what applies to the guide.)

1. First of all, try to use `getaddrinfo()` to get all the `struct sockaddr` info, instead of packing the structures by hand. This will keep you IP version-agnostic, and will eliminate many of the subsequent steps.

2. Any place that you find you're hard-coding anything related to the IP version, try to wrap up in a helper function.

3. Change `AF_INET` to `AF_INET6`.

4. Change `PF_INET` to `PF_INET6`.

5. Change `INADDR_ANY` assignments to `in6addr_any` assignments, which are slightly different:

   ```
   struct sockaddr_in sa;
   struct sockaddr_in6 sa6;

   sa.sin_addr.s_addr = INADDR_ANY;  // use my IPv4 address
   sa6.sin6_addr = in6addr_any; // use my IPv6 address
   ```

   Also, the value `IN6ADDR_ANY_INIT` can be used as an initializer when the `struct in6_addr` is declared, like so:

   ```
   struct in6_addr ia6 = IN6ADDR_ANY_INIT;
   ```

6. Instead of `struct sockaddr_in` use `struct sockaddr_in6`, being sure to add "6" to the fields as appropriate (see `structs`, above). There is no `sin6_zero` field.

7. Instead of `struct in_addr` use `struct in6_addr`, being sure to add "6" to the fields as appropriate (see `structs`, above).

25

8. Instead of `inet_aton()` or `inet_addr()`, use `inet_pton()`.

9. Instead of `inet_ntoa()`, use `inet_ntop()`.

10. Instead of `gethostbyname()`, use the superior `getaddrinfo()`.

11. Instead of `gethostbyaddr()`, use the superior `getnameinfo()` (although `gethostbyaddr()` can still work with IPv6).

12. `INADDR_BROADCAST` no longer works. Use IPv6 multicast instead.

Et voila!

System Calls or Bust

This is the section where we get into the system calls (and other library calls) that allow you to access the network functionality of a Unix box, or any box that supports the sockets API for that matter (BSD, Windows, Linux, Mac, what-have-you.) When you call one of these functions, the kernel takes over and does all the work for you automagically.

The place most people get stuck around here is what order to call these things in. In that, the man pages are no use, as you've probably discovered. Well, to help with that dreadful situation, I've tried to lay out the system calls in the following sections in *exactly* (approximately) the same order that you'll need to call them in your programs.

That, coupled with a few pieces of sample code here and there, some milk and cookies (which I fear you will have to supply yourself), and some raw guts and courage, and you'll be beaming data around the Internet like the Son of Jon Postel!

(Please note that for brevity, many code snippets below do not include necessary error checking. And they very commonly assume that the result from calls to getaddrinfo() succeed and return a valid entry in the linked list. Both of these situations are properly addressed in the stand-alone programs, though, so use those as a model.)

getaddrinfo()—Prepare to launch!

This is a real workhorse of a function with a lot of options, but usage is actually pretty simple. It helps set up the `structs` you need later on.

A tiny bit of history: it used to be that you would use a function called `gethostbyname()` to do DNS lookups. Then you'd load that information by hand into a `struct sockaddr_in`, and use that in your calls.

This is no longer necessary, thankfully. (Nor is it desirable, if you want to write code that works for both IPv4 and IPv6!) In these modern times, you now have the function `getaddrinfo()` that does all kinds of good stuff for you, including DNS and service name lookups, and fills out the `structs` you need, besides!

Let's take a look!

27

```
#include <sys/types.h>
#include <sys/socket.h>
#include <netdb.h>

int getaddrinfo(const char *node,      // e.g. "www.example.com" or IP
                const char *service,   // e.g. "http" or port number
                const struct addrinfo *hints,
                struct addrinfo **res);
```

You give this function three input parameters, and it gives you a pointer to a linked-list, `res`, of results.

The `node` parameter is the host name to connect to, or an IP address.

Next is the parameter `service`, which can be a port number, like "80", or the name of a particular service (found in The IANA Port List[20] or the `/etc/services` file on your Unix machine) like "http" or "ftp" or "telnet" or "smtp" or whatever.

Finally, the `hints` parameter points to a `struct addrinfo` that you've already filled out with relevant information.

Here's a sample call if you're a server who wants to listen on your host's IP address, port 3490. Note that this doesn't actually do any listening or network setup; it merely sets up structures we'll use later:

```
1   int status;
2   struct addrinfo hints;
3   struct addrinfo *servinfo;  // will point to the results
4
5   memset(&hints, 0, sizeof hints); // make sure the struct is empty
6   hints.ai_family = AF_UNSPEC;       // don't care IPv4 or IPv6
7   hints.ai_socktype = SOCK_STREAM; // TCP stream sockets
8   hints.ai_flags = AI_PASSIVE;      // fill in my IP for me
9
10  if ((status = getaddrinfo(NULL, "3490", &hints, &servinfo)) != 0) {
11      fprintf(stderr, "getaddrinfo error: %s\n", gai_strerror(status));
12      exit(1);
13  }
14
15  // servinfo now points to a linked list of 1 or more struct addrinfos
16
17  // ... do everything until you don't need servinfo anymore ....
18
19  freeaddrinfo(servinfo); // free the linked-list
```

---

[20]https://www.iana.org/assignments/port-numbers

Notice that I set the `ai_family` to `AF_UNSPEC`, thereby saying that I don't care if we use IPv4 or IPv6. You can set it to `AF_INET` or `AF_INET6` if you want one or the other specifically.

Also, you'll see the `AI_PASSIVE` flag in there; this tells `getaddrinfo()` to assign the address of my local host to the socket structures. This is nice because then you don't have to hardcode it. (Or you can put a specific address in as the first parameter to `getaddrinfo()` where I currently have `NULL`, up there.)

Then we make the call. If there's an error (`getaddrinfo()` returns non-zero), we can print it out using the function `gai_strerror()`, as you see. If everything works properly, though, `servinfo` will point to a linked list of `struct addrinfos`, each of which contains a `struct sockaddr` of some kind that we can use later! Nifty!

Finally, when we're eventually all done with the linked list that `getaddrinfo()` so graciously allocated for us, we can (and should) free it all up with a call to `freeaddrinfo()`.

Here's a sample call if you're a client who wants to connect to a particular server, say "www.example.net" port 3490. Again, this doesn't actually connect, but it sets up the structures we'll use later:

```
int status;
struct addrinfo hints;
struct addrinfo *servinfo;  // will point to the results

memset(&hints, 0, sizeof hints); // make sure the struct is empty
hints.ai_family = AF_UNSPEC;      // don't care IPv4 or IPv6
hints.ai_socktype = SOCK_STREAM; // TCP stream sockets

// get ready to connect
status = getaddrinfo("www.example.net", "3490", &hints, &servinfo);

// servinfo now points to a linked list of 1 or more struct addrinfos

// etc.
```

I keep saying that `servinfo` is a linked list with all kinds of address information. Let's write a quick demo program to show off this information. This short program[21] will print the IP addresses for whatever host you specify on the command line:

```
/*
** showip.c -- show IP addresses for a host given on the command line
*/

#include <stdio.h>
```

---

[21] https://beej.us/guide/bgnet/examples/showip.c

```c
#include <string.h>
#include <sys/types.h>
#include <sys/socket.h>
#include <netdb.h>
#include <arpa/inet.h>
#include <netinet/in.h>

int main(int argc, char *argv[])
{
    struct addrinfo hints, *res, *p;
    int status;
    char ipstr[INET6_ADDRSTRLEN];

    if (argc != 2) {
        fprintf(stderr,"usage: showip hostname\n");
        return 1;
    }

    memset(&hints, 0, sizeof hints);
    hints.ai_family = AF_UNSPEC; // AF_INET or AF_INET6 to force version
    hints.ai_socktype = SOCK_STREAM;

    if ((status = getaddrinfo(argv[1], NULL, &hints, &res)) != 0) {
        fprintf(stderr, "getaddrinfo: %s\n", gai_strerror(status));
        return 2;
    }

    printf("IP addresses for %s:\n\n", argv[1]);

    for(p = res;p != NULL; p = p->ai_next) {
        void *addr;
        char *ipver;

        // get the pointer to the address itself,
        // different fields in IPv4 and IPv6:
        if (p->ai_family == AF_INET) { // IPv4
            struct sockaddr_in *ipv4 = (struct sockaddr_in *)p->ai_addr;
            addr = &(ipv4->sin_addr);
            ipver = "IPv4";
        } else { // IPv6
            struct sockaddr_in6 *ipv6 = (struct sockaddr_in6 *)p->ai_addr;
            addr = &(ipv6->sin6_addr);
            ipver = "IPv6";
```

```
49              }
50
51              // convert the IP to a string and print it:
52              inet_ntop(p->ai_family, addr, ipstr, sizeof ipstr);
53              printf("  %s: %s\n", ipver, ipstr);
54          }
55
56      freeaddrinfo(res); // free the linked list
57
58      return 0;
59  }
```

As you see, the code calls `getaddrinfo()` on whatever you pass on the command line, that fills out the linked list pointed to by `res`, and then we can iterate over the list and print stuff out or do whatever.

(There's a little bit of ugliness there where we have to dig into the different types of `struct sockaddrs` depending on the IP version. Sorry about that! I'm not sure of a better way around it.)

Sample run! Everyone loves screenshots:

```
$ showip www.example.net
IP addresses for www.example.net:

    IPv4: 192.0.2.88

$ showip ipv6.example.com
IP addresses for ipv6.example.com:

    IPv4: 192.0.2.101
    IPv6: 2001:db8:8c00:22::171
```

Now that we have that under control, we'll use the results we get from `getaddrinfo()` to pass to other socket functions and, at long last, get our network connection established! Keep reading!

socket( )—Get the File Descriptor!

I guess I can put it off no longer—I have to talk about the `socket()` system call. Here's the breakdown:

```
#include <sys/types.h>
#include <sys/socket.h>

int socket(int domain, int type, int protocol);
```

But what are these arguments? They allow you to say what kind of socket you want (IPv4 or IPv6, stream or datagram, and TCP or UDP).

It used to be people would hardcode these values, and you can absolutely still do that. (domain is PF_INET or PF_INET6, type is SOCK_STREAM or SOCK_DGRAM, and proto- col can be set to 0 to choose the proper protocol for the given type. Or you can call getprotobyname() to look up the protocol you want, "tcp" or "udp".)

(This PF_INET thing is a close relative of the AF_INET that you can use when initializing the sin_family field in your struct sockaddr_in. In fact, they're so closely related that they actually have the same value, and many programmers will call socket() and pass AF_INET as the first argument instead of PF_INET. Now, get some milk and cookies, because it's time for a story. Once upon a time, a long time ago, it was thought that maybe an address family (what the "AF" in "AF_INET" stands for) might support several protocols that were referred to by their protocol family (what the "PF" in "PF_INET" stands for). That didn't happen. And they all lived happily ever after, The End. So the most correct thing to do is to use AF_INET in your struct sockaddr_in and PF_INET in your call to socket().)

Anyway, enough of that. What you really want to do is use the values from the results of the call to getaddrinfo(), and feed them into socket() directly like this:

```
1   int s;
2   struct addrinfo hints, *res;
3
4   // do the lookup
5   // [pretend we already filled out the "hints" struct]
6   getaddrinfo("www.example.com", "http", &hints, &res);
7
8   // again, you should do error-checking on getaddrinfo(), and walk
9   // the "res" linked list looking for valid entries instead of just
10  // assuming the first one is good (like many of these examples do).
11  // See the section on client/server for real examples.
12
13  s = socket(res->ai_family, res->ai_socktype, res->ai_protocol);
```

socket() simply returns to you a *socket descriptor* that you can use in later system calls, or -1 on error. The global variable errno is set to the error's value (see the errno man page for more details, and a quick note on using errno in multithreaded programs).

Fine, fine, fine, but what good is this socket? The answer is that it's really no good by itself, and you need to read on and make more system calls for it to make any sense.

bind( )—What port am I on?

Once you have a socket, you might have to associate that socket with a port on your local machine. (This is commonly done if you're going to `listen( )` for incoming connections on a specific port—multiplayer network games do this when they tell you to "connect to 192.168.5.10 port 3490".) The port number is used by the kernel to match an incoming packet to a certain process's socket descriptor. If you're going to only be doing a `connect( )` (because you're the client, not the server), this is probably be unnecessary. Read it anyway, just for kicks.

Here is the synopsis for the `bind( )` system call:

```
#include <sys/types.h>
#include <sys/socket.h>

int bind(int sockfd, struct sockaddr *my_addr, int addrlen);
```

`sockfd` is the socket file descriptor returned by `socket( )`. `my_addr` is a pointer to a `struct sockaddr` that contains information about your address, namely, port and IP address. `addrlen` is the length in bytes of that address.

Whew. That's a bit to absorb in one chunk. Let's have an example that binds the socket to the host the program is running on, port 3490:

```
1   struct addrinfo hints, *res;
2   int sockfd;
3
4   // first, load up address structs with getaddrinfo():
5
6   memset(&hints, 0, sizeof hints);
7   hints.ai_family = AF_UNSPEC;   // use IPv4 or IPv6, whichever
8   hints.ai_socktype = SOCK_STREAM;
9   hints.ai_flags = AI_PASSIVE;     // fill in my IP for me
10
11  getaddrinfo(NULL, "3490", &hints, &res);
12
13  // make a socket:
14
15  sockfd = socket(res->ai_family, res->ai_socktype, res->ai_protocol);
16
17  // bind it to the port we passed in to getaddrinfo():
18
19  bind(sockfd, res->ai_addr, res->ai_addrlen);
```

By using the `AI_PASSIVE` flag, I'm telling the program to bind to the IP of the host it's running on. If you want to bind to a specific local IP address, drop the `AI_PASSIVE` and put an IP address in for the first argument to `getaddrinfo()`.

`bind()` also returns `-1` on error and sets `errno` to the error's value.

Lots of old code manually packs the `struct sockaddr_in` before calling `bind()`. Obviously this is IPv4-specific, but there's really nothing stopping you from doing the same thing with IPv6, except that using `getaddrinfo()` is going to be easier, generally. Anyway, the old code looks something like this:

```
// !!! THIS IS THE OLD WAY !!!

int sockfd;
struct sockaddr_in my_addr;

sockfd = socket(PF_INET, SOCK_STREAM, 0);

my_addr.sin_family = AF_INET;
my_addr.sin_port = htons(MYPORT);     // short, network byte order
my_addr.sin_addr.s_addr = inet_addr("10.12.110.57");
memset(my_addr.sin_zero, '\0', sizeof my_addr.sin_zero);

bind(sockfd, (struct sockaddr *)&my_addr, sizeof my_addr);
```

In the above code, you could also assign `INADDR_ANY` to the `s_addr` field if you wanted to bind to your local IP address (like the `AI_PASSIVE` flag, above). The IPv6 version of `INADDR_ANY` is a global variable `in6addr_any` that is assigned into the `sin6_addr` field of your `struct sockaddr_in6`. (There is also a macro `IN6ADDR_ANY_INIT` that you can use in a variable initializer.)

Another thing to watch out for when calling `bind()`: don't go underboard with your port numbers. All ports below 1024 are RESERVED (unless you're the superuser)! You can have any port number above that, right up to 65535 (provided they aren't already being used by another program).

Sometimes, you might notice, you try to rerun a server and `bind()` fails, claiming "Address already in use." What does that mean? Well, a little bit of a socket that was connected is still hanging around in the kernel, and it's hogging the port. You can either wait for it to clear (a minute or so), or add code to your program allowing it to reuse the port, like this:

```
int yes=1;
//char yes='1'; // Solaris people use this

// lose the pesky "Address already in use" error message
if (setsockopt(listener,SOL_SOCKET,SO_REUSEADDR,&yes,sizeof yes) == -1) {
    perror("setsockopt");
    exit(1);
}
```

One small extra final note about bind( ): there are times when you won't absolutely have to call it. If you are connect( )ing to a remote machine and you don't care what your local port is (as is the case with telnet where you only care about the remote port), you can simply call connect( ), it'll check to see if the socket is unbound, and will bind( ) it to an unused local port if necessary.

connect( )—Hey, you!

Let's just pretend for a few minutes that you're a telnet application. Your user commands you (just like in the movie *TRON*) to get a socket file descriptor. You comply and call socket( ). Next, the user tells you to connect to "10.12.110.57" on port "23" (the standard telnet port). Yow! What do you do now?

Lucky for you, program, you're now perusing the section on connect( )—how to connect to a remote host. So read furiously onward! No time to lose!

The connect( ) call is as follows:

```
#include <sys/types.h>
#include <sys/socket.h>

int connect(int sockfd, struct sockaddr *serv_addr, int addrlen);
```

sockfd is our friendly neighborhood socket file descriptor, as returned by the socket( ) call, serv_addr is a struct sockaddr containing the destination port and IP address, and addrlen is the length in bytes of the server address structure.

All of this information can be gleaned from the results of the getaddrinfo( ) call, which rocks.

Is this starting to make more sense? I can't hear you from here, so I'll just have to hope that it is. Let's have an example where we make a socket connection to "www.example.com", port 3490:

```
1   struct addrinfo hints, *res;
2   int sockfd;
3
4   // first, load up address structs with getaddrinfo():
5
6   memset(&hints, 0, sizeof hints);
7   hints.ai_family = AF_UNSPEC;
8   hints.ai_socktype = SOCK_STREAM;
9
10  getaddrinfo("www.example.com", "3490", &hints, &res);
11
12  // make a socket:
```

```
13
14   sockfd = socket(res->ai_family, res->ai_socktype, res->ai_protocol);
15
16   // connect!
17
18   connect(sockfd, res->ai_addr, res->ai_addrlen);
```

Again, old-school programs filled out their own struct sockaddr_ins to pass to connect(). You can do that if you want to. See the similar note in the bind() section, above.

Be sure to check the return value from connect()—it'll return -1 on error and set the variable errno.

Also, notice that we didn't call bind(). Basically, we don't care about our local port number; we only care where we're going (the remote port). The kernel will choose a local port for us, and the site we connect to will automatically get this information from us. No worries.

listen()—Will somebody please call me?

Ok, time for a change of pace. What if you don't want to connect to a remote host. Say, just for kicks, that you want to wait for incoming connections and handle them in some way. The process is two step: first you listen(), then you accept() (see below).

The listen call is fairly simple, but requires a bit of explanation:

```
int listen(int sockfd, int backlog);
```

sockfd is the usual socket file descriptor from the socket() system call. backlog is the number of connections allowed on the incoming queue. What does that mean? Well, incoming connections are going to wait in this queue until you accept() them (see below) and this is the limit on how many can queue up. Most systems silently limit this number to about 20; you can probably get away with setting it to 5 or 10.

Again, as per usual, listen() returns -1 and sets errno on error.

Well, as you can probably imagine, we need to call bind() before we call listen() so that the server is running on a specific port. (You have to be able to tell your buddies which port to connect to!) So if you're going to be listening for incoming connections, the sequence of system calls you'll make is:

```
1   getaddrinfo();
2   socket();
3   bind();
4   listen();
5   /* accept() goes here */
```

I'll just leave that in the place of sample code, since it's fairly self-explanatory. (The code in the accept( ) section, below, is more complete.) The really tricky part of this whole sha-bang is the call to accept( ).

accept( )—"Thank you for calling port 3490."

Get ready—the accept( ) call is kinda weird! What's going to happen is this: someone far far away will try to connect( ) to your machine on a port that you are listen( )ing on. Their connection will be queued up waiting to be accept( )ed. You call accept( ) and you tell it to get the pending connection. It'll return to you a *brand new socket file descriptor* to use for this single connection! That's right, suddenly you have *two socket file descriptors* for the price of one! The original one is still listening for more new connections, and the newly created one is finally ready to send( ) and recv( ). We're there!

The call is as follows:

```
#include <sys/types.h>
#include <sys/socket.h>

int accept(int sockfd, struct sockaddr *addr, socklen_t *addrlen);
```

sockfd is the listen( )ing socket descriptor. Easy enough. addr will usually be a pointer to a local struct sockaddr_storage. This is where the information about the incoming connection will go (and with it you can determine which host is calling you from which port). addrlen is a local integer variable that should be set to sizeof(struct sockaddr_storage) before its address is passed to accept( ). accept( ) will not put more than that many bytes into addr. If it puts fewer in, it'll change the value of addrlen to reflect that.

Guess what? accept( ) returns -1 and sets errno if an error occurs. Betcha didn't figure that.

Like before, this is a bunch to absorb in one chunk, so here's a sample code fragment for your perusal:

```
1   #include <string.h>
2   #include <sys/types.h>
3   #include <sys/socket.h>
4   #include <netinet/in.h>
5
6   #define MYPORT "3490"   // the port users will be connecting to
7   #define BACKLOG 10      // how many pending connections queue will hold
8
9   int main(void)
10  {
11      struct sockaddr_storage their_addr;
```

```
12      socklen_t addr_size;
13      struct addrinfo hints, *res;
14      int sockfd, new_fd;
15
16      // !! don't forget your error checking for these calls !!
17
18      // first, load up address structs with getaddrinfo():
19
20      memset(&hints, 0, sizeof hints);
21      hints.ai_family = AF_UNSPEC;   // use IPv4 or IPv6, whichever
22      hints.ai_socktype = SOCK_STREAM;
23      hints.ai_flags = AI_PASSIVE;     // fill in my IP for me
24
25      getaddrinfo(NULL, MYPORT, &hints, &res);
26
27      // make a socket, bind it, and listen on it:
28
29      sockfd = socket(res->ai_family, res->ai_socktype, res->ai_protocol);
30      bind(sockfd, res->ai_addr, res->ai_addrlen);
31      listen(sockfd, BACKLOG);
32
33      // now accept an incoming connection:
34
35      addr_size = sizeof their_addr;
36      new_fd = accept(sockfd, (struct sockaddr *)&their_addr, &addr_size);
37
38      // ready to communicate on socket descriptor new_fd!
39      .
40      .
41      .
```

Again, note that we will use the socket descriptor new_fd for all send() and recv() calls. If you're only getting one single connection ever, you can close() the listening sockfd in order to prevent more incoming connections on the same port, if you so desire.

send() and recv()—Talk to me, baby!

These two functions are for communicating over stream sockets or connected datagram sockets. If you want to use regular unconnected datagram sockets, you'll need to see the section on sendto() and recvfrom(), below.

The send() call:

```
int send(int sockfd, const void *msg, int len, int flags);
```

sockfd is the socket descriptor you want to send data to (whether it's the one returned by socket( ) or the one you got with accept( )). msg is a pointer to the data you want to send, and len is the length of that data in bytes. Just set flags to 0. (See the send( ) man page for more information concerning flags.)

Some sample code might be:

```
1  char *msg = "Beej was here!";
2  int len, bytes_sent;
3  .
4  .
5  .
6  len = strlen(msg);
7  bytes_sent = send(sockfd, msg, len, 0);
8  .
9  .
10 .
```

send( ) returns the number of bytes actually sent out—*this might be less than the number you told it to send!* See, sometimes you tell it to send a whole gob of data and it just can't handle it. It'll fire off as much of the data as it can, and trust you to send the rest later. Remember, if the value returned by send( ) doesn't match the value in len, it's up to you to send the rest of the string. The good news is this: if the packet is small (less than 1K or so) it will *probably* manage to send the whole thing all in one go. Again, -1 is returned on error, and errno is set to the error number.

The recv( ) call is similar in many respects:

```
int recv(int sockfd, void *buf, int len, int flags);
```

sockfd is the socket descriptor to read from, buf is the buffer to read the information into, len is the maximum length of the buffer, and flags can again be set to 0. (See the recv( ) man page for flag information.)

recv( ) returns the number of bytes actually read into the buffer, or -1 on error (with errno set, accordingly).

Wait! recv( ) can return 0. This can mean only one thing: the remote side has closed the connection on you! A return value of 0 is recv( )'s way of letting you know this has occurred.

There, that was easy, wasn't it? You can now pass data back and forth on stream sockets! Whee! You're a Unix Network Programmer!

`sendto()` and `recvfrom()`—Talk to me, DGRAM-style

"This is all fine and dandy," I hear you saying, "but where does this leave me with unconnected datagram sockets?" No problemo, amigo. We have just the thing.

Since datagram sockets aren't connected to a remote host, guess which piece of information we need to give before we send a packet? That's right! The destination address! Here's the scoop:

```
int sendto(int sockfd, const void *msg, int len, unsigned int flags,
           const struct sockaddr *to, socklen_t tolen);
```

As you can see, this call is basically the same as the call to `send()` with the addition of two other pieces of information. `to` is a pointer to a `struct sockaddr` (which will probably be another `struct sockaddr_in` or `struct sockaddr_in6` or `struct sockaddr_storage` that you cast at the last minute) which contains the destination IP address and port. `tolen`, an `int` deep-down, can simply be set to `sizeof *to` or `sizeof(struct sockaddr_storage)`.

To get your hands on the destination address structure, you'll probably either get it from `getaddrinfo()`, or from `recvfrom()`, below, or you'll fill it out by hand.

Just like with `send()`, `sendto()` returns the number of bytes actually sent (which, again, might be less than the number of bytes you told it to send!), or `-1` on error.

Equally similar are `recv()` and `recvfrom()`. The synopsis of `recvfrom()` is:

```
int recvfrom(int sockfd, void *buf, int len, unsigned int flags,
             struct sockaddr *from, int *fromlen);
```

Again, this is just like `recv()` with the addition of a couple fields. `from` is a pointer to a local `struct sockaddr_storage` that will be filled with the IP address and port of the originating machine. `fromlen` is a pointer to a local `int` that should be initialized to `sizeof *from` or `sizeof(struct sockaddr_storage)`. When the function returns, `fromlen` will contain the length of the address actually stored in `from`.

`recvfrom()` returns the number of bytes received, or `-1` on error (with `errno` set accordingly).

So, here's a question: why do we use `struct sockaddr_storage` as the socket type? Why not `struct sockaddr_in`? Because, you see, we want to not tie ourselves down to IPv4 or IPv6. So we use the generic `struct sockaddr_storage` which we know will be big enough for either.

(So... here's another question: why isn't `struct sockaddr` itself big enough for any address? We even cast the general-purpose `struct sockaddr_storage` to the general-purpose `struct sockaddr`! Seems extraneous and redundant, huh. The answer is, it just isn't big enough, and I'd guess that changing it at this point would be Problematic. So they made a new one.)

Remember, if you `connect()` a datagram socket, you can then simply use `send()` and `recv()` for all your transactions. The socket itself is still a datagram socket and the packets still use UDP, but the socket interface will automatically add the destination and source information for you.

`close()` and `shutdown()`—Get outta my face!

Whew! You've been `send()`ing and `recv()`ing data all day long, and you've had it. You're ready to close the connection on your socket descriptor. This is easy. You can just use the regular Unix file descriptor `close()` function:

```
close(sockfd);
```

This will prevent any more reads and writes to the socket. Anyone attempting to read or write the socket on the remote end will receive an error.

Just in case you want a little more control over how the socket closes, you can use the `shutdown()` function. It allows you to cut off communication in a certain direction, or both ways (just like `close()` does). Synopsis:

```
int shutdown(int sockfd, int how);
```

`sockfd` is the socket file descriptor you want to shutdown, and `how` is one of the following:

how	Effect
0	Further receives are disallowed
1	Further sends are disallowed
2	Further sends and receives are disallowed (like `close()`)

`shutdown()` returns 0 on success, and -1 on error (with `errno` set accordingly).

If you deign to use `shutdown()` on unconnected datagram sockets, it will simply make the socket unavailable for further `send()` and `recv()` calls (remember that you can use these if you `connect()` your datagram socket).

It's important to note that `shutdown()` doesn't actually close the file descriptor—it just changes its usability. To free a socket descriptor, you need to use `close()`.

Nothing to it.

(Except to remember that if you're using Windows and Winsock that you should call `closesocket()` instead of `close()`.)

getpeername()—Who are you?

This function is so easy.

It's so easy, I almost didn't give it its own section. But here it is anyway.

The function getpeername() will tell you who is at the other end of a connected stream socket. The synopsis:

```
#include <sys/socket.h>

int getpeername(int sockfd, struct sockaddr *addr, int *addrlen);
```

sockfd is the descriptor of the connected stream socket, addr is a pointer to a struct sockaddr (or a struct sockaddr_in) that will hold the information about the other side of the connection, and addrlen is a pointer to an int, that should be initialized to sizeof *addr or sizeof(struct sockaddr).

The function returns -1 on error and sets errno accordingly.

Once you have their address, you can use inet_ntop(), getnameinfo(), or gethostbyaddr() to print or get more information. No, you can't get their login name. (Ok, ok. If the other computer is running an ident daemon, this is possible. This, however, is beyond the scope of this document. Check out RFC 1413[22] for more info.)

gethostname()—Who am I?

Even easier than getpeername() is the function gethostname(). It returns the name of the computer that your program is running on. The name can then be used by gethostbyname(), below, to determine the IP address of your local machine.

What could be more fun? I could think of a few things, but they don't pertain to socket programming. Anyway, here's the breakdown:

```
#include <unistd.h>

int gethostname(char *hostname, size_t size);
```

The arguments are simple: hostname is a pointer to an array of chars that will contain the hostname upon the function's return, and size is the length in bytes of the hostname array.

The function returns 0 on successful completion, and -1 on error, setting errno as usual.

---

[22]https://tools.ietf.org/html/rfc1413

Client-Server Background

It's a client-server world, baby. Just about everything on the network deals with client processes talking to server processes and vice-versa. Take telnet, for instance. When you connect to a remote host on port 23 with telnet (the client), a program on that host (called telnetd, the server) springs to life. It handles the incoming telnet connection, sets you up with a login prompt, etc.

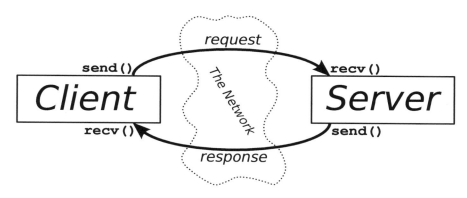

Figure 2: Client-Server Interaction.

The exchange of information between client and server is summarized in the above diagram.

Note that the client-server pair can speak SOCK_STREAM, SOCK_DGRAM, or anything else (as long as they're speaking the same thing). Some good examples of client-server pairs are telnet/telnetd, ftp/ftpd, or Firefox/Apache. Every time you use ftp, there's a remote program, ftpd, that serves you.

Often, there will only be one server on a machine, and that server will handle multiple clients using fork(). The basic routine is: server will wait for a connection, accept() it, and fork() a child process to handle it. This is what our sample server does in the next section.

43

A Simple Stream Server

All this server does is send the string "`Hello, world!`" out over a stream connection. All you need to do to test this server is run it in one window, and telnet to it from another with:

```
$ telnet remotehostname 3490
```

where `remotehostname` is the name of the machine you're running it on.

The server code[23]:

```
1   /*
2   ** server.c -- a stream socket server demo
3   */
4
5   #include <stdio.h>
6   #include <stdlib.h>
7   #include <unistd.h>
8   #include <errno.h>
9   #include <string.h>
10  #include <sys/types.h>
11  #include <sys/socket.h>
12  #include <netinet/in.h>
13  #include <netdb.h>
14  #include <arpa/inet.h>
15  #include <sys/wait.h>
16  #include <signal.h>
17
18  #define PORT "3490"  // the port users will be connecting to
19
20  #define BACKLOG 10   // how many pending connections queue will hold
21
22  void sigchld_handler(int s)
23  {
24      // waitpid() might overwrite errno, so we save and restore it:
25      int saved_errno = errno;
26
27      while(waitpid(-1, NULL, WNOHANG) > 0);
28
29      errno = saved_errno;
30  }
31
32
33  // get sockaddr, IPv4 or IPv6:
```

---

[23]https://beej.us/guide/bgnet/examples/server.c

```
34   void *get_in_addr(struct sockaddr *sa)
35   {
36       if (sa->sa_family == AF_INET) {
37           return &(((struct sockaddr_in*)sa)->sin_addr);
38       }
39
40       return &(((struct sockaddr_in6*)sa)->sin6_addr);
41   }
42
43   int main(void)
44   {
45       int sockfd, new_fd;  // listen on sock_fd, new connection on new_fd
46       struct addrinfo hints, *servinfo, *p;
47       struct sockaddr_storage their_addr; // connector's address information
48       socklen_t sin_size;
49       struct sigaction sa;
50       int yes=1;
51       char s[INET6_ADDRSTRLEN];
52       int rv;
53
54       memset(&hints, 0, sizeof hints);
55       hints.ai_family = AF_UNSPEC;
56       hints.ai_socktype = SOCK_STREAM;
57       hints.ai_flags = AI_PASSIVE; // use my IP
58
59       if ((rv = getaddrinfo(NULL, PORT, &hints, &servinfo)) != 0) {
60           fprintf(stderr, "getaddrinfo: %s\n", gai_strerror(rv));
61           return 1;
62       }
63
64       // loop through all the results and bind to the first we can
65       for(p = servinfo; p != NULL; p = p->ai_next) {
66           if ((sockfd = socket(p->ai_family, p->ai_socktype,
67                   p->ai_protocol)) == -1) {
68               perror("server: socket");
69               continue;
70           }
71
72           if (setsockopt(sockfd, SOL_SOCKET, SO_REUSEADDR, &yes,
73                   sizeof(int)) == -1) {
74               perror("setsockopt");
75               exit(1);
76           }
```

```
77
78          if (bind(sockfd, p->ai_addr, p->ai_addrlen) == -1) {
79              close(sockfd);
80              perror("server: bind");
81              continue;
82          }
83
84          break;
85      }
86
87      freeaddrinfo(servinfo); // all done with this structure
88
89      if (p == NULL)  {
90          fprintf(stderr, "server: failed to bind\n");
91          exit(1);
92      }
93
94      if (listen(sockfd, BACKLOG) == -1) {
95          perror("listen");
96          exit(1);
97      }
98
99      sa.sa_handler = sigchld_handler; // reap all dead processes
100     sigemptyset(&sa.sa_mask);
101     sa.sa_flags = SA_RESTART;
102     if (sigaction(SIGCHLD, &sa, NULL) == -1) {
103         perror("sigaction");
104         exit(1);
105     }
106
107     printf("server: waiting for connections...\n");
108
109     while(1) {  // main accept() loop
110         sin_size = sizeof their_addr;
111         new_fd = accept(sockfd, (struct sockaddr *)&their_addr, &sin_size);
112         if (new_fd == -1) {
113             perror("accept");
114             continue;
115         }
116
117         inet_ntop(their_addr.ss_family,
118             get_in_addr((struct sockaddr *)&their_addr),
119             s, sizeof s);
```

```
120         printf("server: got connection from %s\n", s);
121
122         if (!fork()) { // this is the child process
123             close(sockfd); // child doesn't need the listener
124             if (send(new_fd, "Hello, world!", 13, 0) == -1)
125                 perror("send");
126             close(new_fd);
127             exit(0);
128         }
129         close(new_fd);   // parent doesn't need this
130     }
131
132     return 0;
133 }
```

In case you're curious, I have the code in one big `main()` function for (I feel) syntactic clarity. Feel free to split it into smaller functions if it makes you feel better.

(Also, this whole `sigaction()` thing might be new to you—that's ok. The code that's there is responsible for reaping zombie processes that appear as the `fork()`ed child processes exit. If you make lots of zombies and don't reap them, your system administrator will become agitated.)

You can get the data from this server by using the client listed in the next section.

A Simple Stream Client

This guy's even easier than the server. All this client does is connect to the host you specify on the command line, port 3490. It gets the string that the server sends.

The client source[24]:

```
1  /*
2  ** client.c -- a stream socket client demo
3  */
4
5  #include <stdio.h>
6  #include <stdlib.h>
7  #include <unistd.h>
8  #include <errno.h>
9  #include <string.h>
10 #include <netdb.h>
11 #include <sys/types.h>
12 #include <netinet/in.h>
```

---

[24]https://beej.us/guide/bgnet/examples/client.c

```
13   #include <sys/socket.h>

14

15   #include <arpa/inet.h>

16

17   #define PORT "3490" // the port client will be connecting to

18

19   #define MAXDATASIZE 100 // max number of bytes we can get at once

20

21   // get sockaddr, IPv4 or IPv6:
22   void *get_in_addr(struct sockaddr *sa)
23   {
24       if (sa->sa_family == AF_INET) {
25           return &(((struct sockaddr_in*)sa)->sin_addr);
26       }

27

28       return &(((struct sockaddr_in6*)sa)->sin6_addr);
29   }

30

31   int main(int argc, char *argv[])
32   {
33       int sockfd, numbytes;
34       char buf[MAXDATASIZE];
35       struct addrinfo hints, *servinfo, *p;
36       int rv;
37       char s[INET6_ADDRSTRLEN];

38

39       if (argc != 2) {
40           fprintf(stderr,"usage: client hostname\n");
41           exit(1);
42       }

43

44       memset(&hints, 0, sizeof hints);
45       hints.ai_family = AF_UNSPEC;
46       hints.ai_socktype = SOCK_STREAM;

47

48       if ((rv = getaddrinfo(argv[1], PORT, &hints, &servinfo)) != 0) {
49           fprintf(stderr, "getaddrinfo: %s\n", gai_strerror(rv));
50           return 1;
51       }

52

53       // loop through all the results and connect to the first we can
54       for(p = servinfo; p != NULL; p = p->ai_next) {
55           if ((sockfd = socket(p->ai_family, p->ai_socktype,
```

```
56                     p->ai_protocol)) == -1) {
57                 perror("client: socket");
58                 continue;
59             }
60
61             if (connect(sockfd, p->ai_addr, p->ai_addrlen) == -1) {
62                 close(sockfd);
63                 perror("client: connect");
64                 continue;
65             }
66
67             break;
68         }
69
70         if (p == NULL) {
71             fprintf(stderr, "client: failed to connect\n");
72             return 2;
73         }
74
75         inet_ntop(p->ai_family, get_in_addr((struct sockaddr *)p->ai_addr),
76                 s, sizeof s);
77         printf("client: connecting to %s\n", s);
78
79         freeaddrinfo(servinfo); // all done with this structure
80
81         if ((numbytes = recv(sockfd, buf, MAXDATASIZE-1, 0)) == -1) {
82             perror("recv");
83             exit(1);
84         }
85
86         buf[numbytes] = '\0';
87
88         printf("client: received '%s'\n",buf);
89
90         close(sockfd);
91
92         return 0;
93     }
```

Notice that if you don't run the server before you run the client, `connect()` returns "Connection refused". Very useful.

Datagram Sockets

We've already covered the basics of UDP datagram sockets with our discussion of
`sendto()` and `recvfrom()`, above, so I'll just present a couple of sample programs:
`talker.c` and `listener.c`.

`listener` sits on a machine waiting for an incoming packet on port 4950. `talker` sends a
packet to that port, on the specified machine, that contains whatever the user enters on the
command line.

Here is the source for `listener.c`[25]:

```c
/*
** listener.c -- a datagram sockets "server" demo
*/

#include <stdio.h>
#include <stdlib.h>
#include <unistd.h>
#include <errno.h>
#include <string.h>
#include <sys/types.h>
#include <sys/socket.h>
#include <netinet/in.h>
#include <arpa/inet.h>
#include <netdb.h>

#define MYPORT "4950"    // the port users will be connecting to

#define MAXBUFLEN 100

// get sockaddr, IPv4 or IPv6:
void *get_in_addr(struct sockaddr *sa)
{
    if (sa->sa_family == AF_INET) {
        return &(((struct sockaddr_in*)sa)->sin_addr);
    }

    return &(((struct sockaddr_in6*)sa)->sin6_addr);
}

int main(void)
{
    int sockfd;
```

---

[25]https://beej.us/guide/bgnet/examples/listener.c

```
33      struct addrinfo hints, *servinfo, *p;
34      int rv;
35      int numbytes;
36      struct sockaddr_storage their_addr;
37      char buf[MAXBUFLEN];
38      socklen_t addr_len;
39      char s[INET6_ADDRSTRLEN];
40
41      memset(&hints, 0, sizeof hints);
42      hints.ai_family = AF_UNSPEC; // set to AF_INET to force IPv4
43      hints.ai_socktype = SOCK_DGRAM;
44      hints.ai_flags = AI_PASSIVE; // use my IP
45
46      if ((rv = getaddrinfo(NULL, MYPORT, &hints, &servinfo)) != 0) {
47          fprintf(stderr, "getaddrinfo: %s\n", gai_strerror(rv));
48          return 1;
49      }
50
51      // loop through all the results and bind to the first we can
52      for(p = servinfo; p != NULL; p = p->ai_next) {
53          if ((sockfd = socket(p->ai_family, p->ai_socktype,
54                  p->ai_protocol)) == -1) {
55              perror("listener: socket");
56              continue;
57          }
58
59          if (bind(sockfd, p->ai_addr, p->ai_addrlen) == -1) {
60              close(sockfd);
61              perror("listener: bind");
62              continue;
63          }
64
65          break;
66      }
67
68      if (p == NULL) {
69          fprintf(stderr, "listener: failed to bind socket\n");
70          return 2;
71      }
72
73      freeaddrinfo(servinfo);
74
75      printf("listener: waiting to recvfrom...\n");
```

```
76
77      addr_len = sizeof their_addr;
78      if ((numbytes = recvfrom(sockfd, buf, MAXBUFLEN-1 , 0,
79          (struct sockaddr *)&their_addr, &addr_len)) == -1) {
80          perror("recvfrom");
81          exit(1);
82      }
83
84      printf("listener: got packet from %s\n",
85          inet_ntop(their_addr.ss_family,
86              get_in_addr((struct sockaddr *)&their_addr),
87              s, sizeof s));
88      printf("listener: packet is %d bytes long\n", numbytes);
89      buf[numbytes] = '\0';
90      printf("listener: packet contains \"%s\"\n", buf);
91
92      close(sockfd);
93
94      return 0;
95  }
```

Notice that in our call to getaddrinfo() we're finally using SOCK_DGRAM. Also, note that there's no need to listen() or accept(). This is one of the perks of using unconnected datagram sockets!

Next comes the source for talker.c[26]:

```
1   /*
2   ** talker.c -- a datagram "client" demo
3   */
4
5   #include <stdio.h>
6   #include <stdlib.h>
7   #include <unistd.h>
8   #include <errno.h>
9   #include <string.h>
10  #include <sys/types.h>
11  #include <sys/socket.h>
12  #include <netinet/in.h>
13  #include <arpa/inet.h>
14  #include <netdb.h>
15
16  #define SERVERPORT "4950"    // the port users will be connecting to
```

---

[26]https://beej.us/guide/bgnet/examples/talker.c

```
17
18   int main(int argc, char *argv[])
19   {
20       int sockfd;
21       struct addrinfo hints, *servinfo, *p;
22       int rv;
23       int numbytes;
24
25       if (argc != 3) {
26           fprintf(stderr,"usage: talker hostname message\n");
27           exit(1);
28       }
29
30       memset(&hints, 0, sizeof hints);
31       hints.ai_family = AF_UNSPEC;
32       hints.ai_socktype = SOCK_DGRAM;
33
34       if ((rv = getaddrinfo(argv[1], SERVERPORT, &hints, &servinfo)) != 0) {
35           fprintf(stderr, "getaddrinfo: %s\n", gai_strerror(rv));
36           return 1;
37       }
38
39       // loop through all the results and make a socket
40       for(p = servinfo; p != NULL; p = p->ai_next) {
41           if ((sockfd = socket(p->ai_family, p->ai_socktype,
42                   p->ai_protocol)) == -1) {
43               perror("talker: socket");
44               continue;
45           }
46
47           break;
48       }
49
50       if (p == NULL) {
51           fprintf(stderr, "talker: failed to create socket\n");
52           return 2;
53       }
54
55       if ((numbytes = sendto(sockfd, argv[2], strlen(argv[2]), 0,
56               p->ai_addr, p->ai_addrlen)) == -1) {
57           perror("talker: sendto");
58           exit(1);
59       }
```

```
60
61      freeaddrinfo(servinfo);
62
63      printf("talker: sent %d bytes to %s\n", numbytes, argv[1]);
64      close(sockfd);
65
66      return 0;
67  }
```

And that's all there is to it! Run `listener` on some machine, then run `talker` on another. Watch them communicate! Fun G-rated excitement for the entire nuclear family!

You don't even have to run the server this time! You can run `talker` by itself, and it just happily fires packets off into the ether where they disappear if no one is ready with a `recvfrom()` on the other side. Remember: data sent using UDP datagram sockets isn't guaranteed to arrive!

Except for one more tiny detail that I've mentioned many times in the past: connected datagram sockets. I need to talk about this here, since we're in the datagram section of the document. Let's say that `talker` calls `connect()` and specifies the `listener`'s address. From that point on, `talker` may only sent to and receive from the address specified by `connect()`. For this reason, you don't have to use `sendto()` and `recvfrom()`; you can simply use `send()` and `recv()`.

Slightly Advanced Techniques

These aren't *really* advanced, but they're getting out of the more basic levels we've already covered. In fact, if you've gotten this far, you should consider yourself fairly accomplished in the basics of Unix network programming! Congratulations!

So here we go into the brave new world of some of the more esoteric things you might want to learn about sockets. Have at it!

Blocking

Blocking. You've heard about it—now what the heck is it? In a nutshell, "block" is techie jargon for "sleep". You probably noticed that when you run listener, above, it just sits there until a packet arrives. What happened is that it called recvfrom(), there was no data, and so recvfrom() is said to "block" (that is, sleep there) until some data arrives.

Lots of functions block. accept() blocks. All the recv() functions block. The reason they can do this is because they're allowed to. When you first create the socket descriptor with socket(), the kernel sets it to blocking. If you don't want a socket to be blocking, you have to make a call to fcntl():

```
1  #include <unistd.h>
2  #include <fcntl.h>
3  .
4  .
5  .
6  sockfd = socket(PF_INET, SOCK_STREAM, 0);
7  fcntl(sockfd, F_SETFL, O_NONBLOCK);
8  .
9  .
10 .
```

By setting a socket to non-blocking, you can effectively "poll" the socket for information. If you try to read from a non-blocking socket and there's no data there, it's not allowed to block—it will return -1 and errno will be set to EAGAIN or EWOULDBLOCK.

(Wait—it can return EAGAIN *or* EWOULDBLOCK? Which do you check for? The specification doesn't actually specify which your system will return, so for portability, check them both.)

Generally speaking, however, this type of polling is a bad idea. If you put your program in a busy-wait looking for data on the socket, you'll suck up CPU time like it was going out of style. A more elegant solution for checking to see if there's data waiting to be read comes in the following section on poll().

poll()—Synchronous I/O Multiplexing

What you really want to be able to do is somehow monitor a *bunch* of sockets at once and then handle the ones that have data ready. This way you don't have to continously poll all those sockets to see which are ready to read.

> *A word of warning: poll() is horribly slow when it comes to giant numbers of connections. In those circumstances, you'll get better performance out of an event library such as libevent[27] that attempts to use the fastest possible method availabile on your system.*

So how can you avoid polling? Not slightly ironically, you can avoid polling by using the poll() system call. In a nutshell, we're going to ask the operating system to do all the dirty work for us, and just let us know when some data is ready to read on which sockets. In the meantime, our process can go to sleep, saving system resources.

The general gameplan is to keep an array of struct pollfds with information about which socket descriptors we want to monitor, and what kind of events we want to monitor for. The OS will block on the poll() call until one of those events occurs (e.g. "socket ready to read!") or until a user-specified timeout occurs.

Usefully, a listen()ing socket will return "ready to read" when a new incoming connection is ready to be accept()ed.

That's enough banter. How do we use this?

```
#include <poll.h>

int poll(struct pollfd fds[], nfds_t nfds, int timeout);
```

fds is our array of information (which sockets to monitor for what), nfds is the count of elements in the array, and timeout is a timeout in milliseconds. It returns the number of elements in the array that have had an event occur.

Let's have a look at that struct:

---

[27]https://libevent.org/

```
struct pollfd {
    int fd;         // the socket descriptor
    short events;   // bitmap of events we're interested in
    short revents;  // when poll() returns, bitmap of events that occurred
};
```

So we're going to have an array of those, and we'll see the `fd` field for each element to a socket descriptor we're interested in monitoring. And then we'll set the `events` field to indicate the type of events we're interested in.

The `events` field is the bitwise-OR of the following:

Macro	Description
POLLIN	Alert me when data is ready to `recv( )` on this socket.
POLLOUT	Alert me when I can `send( )` data to this socket without blocking.

Once you have your array of `struct pollfds` in order, then you can pass it to `poll( )`, also passing the size of the array, as well as a timeout value in milliseconds. (You can specify a negative timeout to wait forever.)

After `poll( )` returns, you can check the `revents` field to see if `POLLIN` or `POLLOUT` is set, indicating that event occurred.

(There's actually more that you can do with the `poll( )` call. See the `poll( )` man page, below, for more details.)

Here's an example[28] where we'll wait 2.5 seconds for data to be ready to read from standard input, i.e. when you hit RETURN:

```
1   #include <stdio.h>
2   #include <poll.h>
3
4   int main(void)
5   {
6       struct pollfd pfds[1]; // More if you want to monitor more
7
8       pfds[0].fd = 0;          // Standard input
9       pfds[0].events = POLLIN; // Tell me when ready to read
10
11      // If you needed to monitor other things, as well:
12      //pfds[1].fd = some_socket; // Some socket descriptor
13      //pfds[1].events = POLLIN;  // Tell me when ready to read
14
```

---

[28]https://beej.us/guide/bgnet/examples/poll.c

```
15      printf("Hit RETURN or wait 2.5 seconds for timeout\n");
16
17      int num_events = poll(pfds, 1, 2500); // 2.5 second timeout
18
19      if (num_events == 0) {
20          printf("Poll timed out!\n");
21      } else {
22          int pollin_happened = pfds[0].revents & POLLIN;
23
24          if (pollin_happened) {
25              printf("File descriptor %d is ready to read\n", pfds[0].fd);
26          } else {
27              printf("Unexpected event occurred: %d\n", pfds[0].revents);
28          }
29      }
30
31      return 0;
32  }
```

Notice again that poll() returns the number of elements in the pfds array for which events have occurred. It doesn't tell you *which* elements in the array (you still have to scan for that), but it does tell you how many entries have a non-zero revents field (so you can stop scanning after you find that many).

A couple questions might come up here: how to I add new file descriptors to the set I pass to poll()? For this, simply make sure you have enough space in the array for all you need, or realloc() more space as needed.

What about deleting items from the set? For this, you can copy the last element in the array over-top the one you're deleting. And then pass in one fewer as the count to poll(). Another option is that you can set any fd field to a negative number and poll() will ignore it.

How can we put it all together into a chat server that you can telnet to?

What we'll do is start a listener socket, and add it to the set of file descriptors to poll(). (It will show ready-to-read when there's an incoming connection.)

Then we'll add new connections to our struct pollfd array. And we'll grow it dynamically if we run out of space.

When a connection is closed, we'll remove it from the array.

And when a connection is ready-to-read, we'll read the data from it and send that data to all the other connections so they can see what the other users typed.

So give this poll server[29] a try. Run it in one window, then `telnet localhost 9034` from a number of other terminal windows. You should be able to see what you type in one window in the other ones (after you hit RETURN).

Not only that, but if you hit `CTRL-]` and type `quit` to exit `telnet`, the server should detect the disconnection and remove you from the array of file descriptors.

```
1   /*
2   ** pollserver.c -- a cheezy multiperson chat server
3   */
4
5   #include <stdio.h>
6   #include <stdlib.h>
7   #include <string.h>
8   #include <unistd.h>
9   #include <sys/types.h>
10  #include <sys/socket.h>
11  #include <netinet/in.h>
12  #include <arpa/inet.h>
13  #include <netdb.h>
14  #include <poll.h>
15
16  #define PORT "9034"    // Port we're listening on
17
18  // Get sockaddr, IPv4 or IPv6:
19  void *get_in_addr(struct sockaddr *sa)
20  {
21      if (sa->sa_family == AF_INET) {
22          return &(((struct sockaddr_in*)sa)->sin_addr);
23      }
24
25      return &(((struct sockaddr_in6*)sa)->sin6_addr);
26  }
27
28  // Return a listening socket
29  int get_listener_socket(void)
30  {
31      int listener;      // Listening socket descriptor
32      int yes=1;         // For setsockopt() SO_REUSEADDR, below
33      int rv;
34
35      struct addrinfo hints, *ai, *p;
36
```

---

[29]https://beej.us/guide/bgnet/examples/pollserver.c

```
37          // Get us a socket and bind it
38          memset(&hints, 0, sizeof hints);
39          hints.ai_family = AF_UNSPEC;
40          hints.ai_socktype = SOCK_STREAM;
41          hints.ai_flags = AI_PASSIVE;
42          if ((rv = getaddrinfo(NULL, PORT, &hints, &ai)) != 0) {
43              fprintf(stderr, "selectserver: %s\n", gai_strerror(rv));
44              exit(1);
45          }
46
47          for(p = ai; p != NULL; p = p->ai_next) {
48              listener = socket(p->ai_family, p->ai_socktype, p->ai_protocol);
49              if (listener < 0) {
50                  continue;
51              }
52
53              // Lose the pesky "address already in use" error message
54              setsockopt(listener, SOL_SOCKET, SO_REUSEADDR, &yes, sizeof(int));
55
56              if (bind(listener, p->ai_addr, p->ai_addrlen) < 0) {
57                  close(listener);
58                  continue;
59              }
60
61              break;
62          }
63
64          // If we got here, it means we didn't get bound
65          if (p == NULL) {
66              return -1;
67          }
68
69          freeaddrinfo(ai); // All done with this
70
71          // Listen
72          if (listen(listener, 10) == -1) {
73              return -1;
74          }
75
76          return listener;
77      }
78
79  // Add a new file descriptor to the set
```

```
80  void add_to_pfds(struct pollfd *pfds[], int newfd, int *fd_count, int *fd_size)
81  {
82      // If we don't have room, add more space in the pfds array
83      if (*fd_count == *fd_size) {
84          *fd_size *= 2; // Double it
85
86          *pfds = realloc(*pfds, sizeof(**pfds) * (*fd_size));
87      }
88
89      (*pfds)[*fd_count].fd = newfd;
90      (*pfds)[*fd_count].events = POLLIN; // Check ready-to-read
91
92      (*fd_count)++;
93  }
94
95  // Remove an index from the set
96  void del_from_pfds(struct pollfd pfds[], int i, int *fd_count)
97  {
98      // Copy the one from the end over this one
99      pfds[i] = pfds[*fd_count-1];
100
101     (*fd_count)--;
102 }
103
104 // Main
105 int main(void)
106 {
107     int listener;      // Listening socket descriptor
108
109     int newfd;         // Newly accept()ed socket descriptor
110     struct sockaddr_storage remoteaddr; // Client address
111     socklen_t addrlen;
112
113     char buf[256];     // Buffer for client data
114
115     char remoteIP[INET6_ADDRSTRLEN];
116
117     // Start off with room for 5 connections
118     // (We'll realloc as necessary)
119     int fd_count = 0;
120     int fd_size = 5;
121     struct pollfd *pfds = malloc(sizeof *pfds * fd_size);
122
```

```
123        // Set up and get a listening socket
124        listener = get_listener_socket();
125
126        if (listener == -1) {
127            fprintf(stderr, "error getting listening socket\n");
128            exit(1);
129        }
130
131        // Add the listener to set
132        pfds[0].fd = listener;
133        pfds[0].events = POLLIN; // Report ready to read on incoming connection
134
135        fd_count = 1; // For the listener
136
137        // Main loop
138        for(;;) {
139            int poll_count = poll(pfds, fd_count, -1);
140
141            if (poll_count == -1) {
142                perror("poll");
143                exit(1);
144            }
145
146            // Run through the existing connections looking for data to read
147            for(int i = 0; i < fd_count; i++) {
148
149                // Check if someone's ready to read
150                if (pfds[i].revents & POLLIN) { // We got one!!
151
152                    if (pfds[i].fd == listener) {
153                        // If listener is ready to read, handle new connection
154
155                        addrlen = sizeof remoteaddr;
156                        newfd = accept(listener,
157                            (struct sockaddr *)&remoteaddr,
158                            &addrlen);
159
160                        if (newfd == -1) {
161                            perror("accept");
162                        } else {
163                            add_to_pfds(&pfds, newfd, &fd_count, &fd_size);
164
165                            printf("pollserver: new connection from %s on "
```

```
166                              "socket %d\n",
167                              inet_ntop(remoteaddr.ss_family,
168                                  get_in_addr((struct sockaddr*)&remoteaddr),
169                                  remoteIP, INET6_ADDRSTRLEN),
170                              newfd);
171                      }
172                  } else {
173                      // If not the listener, we're just a regular client
174                      int nbytes = recv(pfds[i].fd, buf, sizeof buf, 0);
175
176                      int sender_fd = pfds[i].fd;
177
178                      if (nbytes <= 0) {
179                          // Got error or connection closed by client
180                          if (nbytes == 0) {
181                              // Connection closed
182                              printf("pollserver: socket %d hung up\n", sender_fd);
183                          } else {
184                              perror("recv");
185                          }
186
187                          close(pfds[i].fd); // Bye!
188
189                          del_from_pfds(pfds, i, &fd_count);
190
191                      } else {
192                          // We got some good data from a client
193
194                          for(int j = 0; j < fd_count; j++) {
195                              // Send to everyone!
196                              int dest_fd = pfds[j].fd;
197
198                              // Except the listener and ourselves
199                              if (dest_fd != listener && dest_fd != sender_fd) {
200                                  if (send(dest_fd, buf, nbytes, 0) == -1) {
201                                      perror("send");
202                                  }
203                              }
204                          }
205                      }
206                  } // END handle data from client
207              } // END got ready-to-read from poll()
208          } // END looping through file descriptors
```

```
209    } // END for(;;)--and you thought it would never end!
210
211    return 0;
212 }
```

In the next section, we'll look at a similar, older function called `select()`. Both `select()` and `poll()` offer similar functionality and performance, and only really differ in how they're used. `select()` might be slightly more portable, but is perhaps a little clunkier in use. Choose the one you like the best, as long as it's supported on your system.

`select()`—Synchronous I/O Multiplexing, Old School

This function is somewhat strange, but it's very useful. Take the following situation: you are a server and you want to listen for incoming connections as well as keep reading from the connections you already have.

No problem, you say, just an `accept()` and a couple of `recv()`s. Not so fast, buster! What if you're blocking on an `accept()` call? How are you going to `recv()` data at the same time? "Use non-blocking sockets!" No way! You don't want to be a CPU hog. What, then?

`select()` gives you the power to monitor several sockets at the same time. It'll tell you which ones are ready for reading, which are ready for writing, and which sockets have raised exceptions, if you really want to know that.

> *A word of warning:* `select()`, *though very portable, is terribly slow when it comes to giant numbers of connections. In those circumstances, you'll get better performance out of an event library such as libevent[30] that attempts to use the fastest possible method availabile on your system.*

Without any further ado, I'll offer the synopsis of `select()`:

```
#include <sys/time.h>
#include <sys/types.h>
#include <unistd.h>

int select(int numfds, fd_set *readfds, fd_set *writefds,
           fd_set *exceptfds, struct timeval *timeout);
```

The function monitors "sets" of file descriptors; in particular `readfds`, `writefds`, and `exceptfds`. If you want to see if you can read from standard input and some socket descriptor, `sockfd`, just add the file descriptors 0 and `sockfd` to the set `readfds`. The parameter `numfds` should be set to the values of the highest file descriptor plus one. In this example, it should be set to `sockfd+1`, since it is assuredly higher than standard input (0).

---

[30]https://libevent.org/

When `select()` returns, `readfds` will be modified to reflect which of the file descriptors you selected which is ready for reading. You can test them with the macro `FD_ISSET()`, below.

Before progressing much further, I'll talk about how to manipulate these sets. Each set is of the type `fd_set`. The following macros operate on this type:

Function	Description
`FD_SET(int fd, fd_set *set);`	Add `fd` to the set.
`FD_CLR(int fd, fd_set *set);`	Remove `fd` from the set.
`FD_ISSET(int fd, fd_set *set);`	Return true if `fd` is in the set.
`FD_ZERO(fd_set *set);`	Clear all entries from the set.

Finally, what is this weirded out `struct timeval`? Well, sometimes you don't want to wait forever for someone to send you some data. Maybe every 96 seconds you want to print "Still Going…" to the terminal even though nothing has happened. This time structure allows you to specify a timeout period. If the time is exceeded and `select()` still hasn't found any ready file descriptors, it'll return so you can continue processing.

The `struct timeval` has the follow fields:

```
struct timeval {
    int tv_sec;     // seconds
    int tv_usec;    // microseconds
};
```

Just set `tv_sec` to the number of seconds to wait, and set `tv_usec` to the number of microseconds to wait. Yes, that's _micro_seconds, not milliseconds. There are 1,000 microseconds in a millisecond, and 1,000 milliseconds in a second. Thus, there are 1,000,000 microseconds in a second. Why is it "usec"? The "u" is supposed to look like the Greek letter μ (Mu) that we use for "micro". Also, when the function returns, `timeout` *might* be updated to show the time still remaining. This depends on what flavor of Unix you're running.

Yay! We have a microsecond resolution timer! Well, don't count on it. You'll probably have to wait some part of your standard Unix timeslice no matter how small you set your `struct timeval`.

Other things of interest: If you set the fields in your `struct timeval` to 0, `select()` will timeout immediately, effectively polling all the file descriptors in your sets. If you set the parameter `timeout` to NULL, it will never timeout, and will wait until the first file descriptor is ready. Finally, if you don't care about waiting for a certain set, you can just set it to NULL in the call to `select()`.

The following code snippet[31] waits 2.5 seconds for something to appear on standard input:

```
/*
** select.c -- a select() demo
*/

#include <stdio.h>
#include <sys/time.h>
#include <sys/types.h>
#include <unistd.h>

#define STDIN 0  // file descriptor for standard input

int main(void)
{
    struct timeval tv;
    fd_set readfds;

    tv.tv_sec = 2;
    tv.tv_usec = 500000;

    FD_ZERO(&readfds);
    FD_SET(STDIN, &readfds);

    // don't care about writefds and exceptfds:
    select(STDIN+1, &readfds, NULL, NULL, &tv);

    if (FD_ISSET(STDIN, &readfds))
        printf("A key was pressed!\n");
    else
        printf("Timed out.\n");

    return 0;
}
```

If you're on a line buffered terminal, the key you hit should be RETURN or it will time out anyway.

Now, some of you might think this is a great way to wait for data on a datagram socket—and you are right: it *might* be. Some Unices can use select in this manner, and some can't. You should see what your local man page says on the matter if you want to attempt it.

Some Unices update the time in your `struct timeval` to reflect the amount of time still remaining before a timeout. But others do not. Don't rely on that occurring if you want

---

[31] https://beej.us/guide/bgnet/examples/select.c

to be portable. (Use `gettimeofday()` if you need to track time elapsed. It's a bummer, I know, but that's the way it is.)

What happens if a socket in the read set closes the connection? Well, in that case, `select()` returns with that socket descriptor set as "ready to read". When you actually do `recv()` from it, `recv()` will return `0`. That's how you know the client has closed the connection.

One more note of interest about `select()`: if you have a socket that is `listen()`ing, you can check to see if there is a new connection by putting that socket's file descriptor in the `readfds` set.

And that, my friends, is a quick overview of the almighty `select()` function.

But, by popular demand, here is an in-depth example. Unfortunately, the difference between the dirt-simple example, above, and this one here is significant. But have a look, then read the description that follows it.

This program[32] acts like a simple multi-user chat server. Start it running in one window, then `telnet` to it ("`telnet hostname 9034`") from multiple other windows. When you type something in one `telnet` session, it should appear in all the others.

```
1   /*
2   ** selectserver.c -- a cheezy multiperson chat server
3   */
4
5   #include <stdio.h>
6   #include <stdlib.h>
7   #include <string.h>
8   #include <unistd.h>
9   #include <sys/types.h>
10  #include <sys/socket.h>
11  #include <netinet/in.h>
12  #include <arpa/inet.h>
13  #include <netdb.h>
14
15  #define PORT "9034"   // port we're listening on
16
17  // get sockaddr, IPv4 or IPv6:
18  void *get_in_addr(struct sockaddr *sa)
19  {
20      if (sa->sa_family == AF_INET) {
21          return &(((struct sockaddr_in*)sa)->sin_addr);
22      }
23
24      return &(((struct sockaddr_in6*)sa)->sin6_addr);
```

---

[32]https://beej.us/guide/bgnet/examples/selectserver.c

```
25    }
26
27    int main(void)
28    {
29        fd_set master;      // master file descriptor list
30        fd_set read_fds;    // temp file descriptor list for select()
31        int fdmax;          // maximum file descriptor number
32
33        int listener;       // listening socket descriptor
34        int newfd;          // newly accept()ed socket descriptor
35        struct sockaddr_storage remoteaddr; // client address
36        socklen_t addrlen;
37
38        char buf[256];      // buffer for client data
39        int nbytes;
40
41        char remoteIP[INET6_ADDRSTRLEN];
42
43        int yes=1;          // for setsockopt() SO_REUSEADDR, below
44        int i, j, rv;
45
46        struct addrinfo hints, *ai, *p;
47
48        FD_ZERO(&master);    // clear the master and temp sets
49        FD_ZERO(&read_fds);
50
51        // get us a socket and bind it
52        memset(&hints, 0, sizeof hints);
53        hints.ai_family = AF_UNSPEC;
54        hints.ai_socktype = SOCK_STREAM;
55        hints.ai_flags = AI_PASSIVE;
56        if ((rv = getaddrinfo(NULL, PORT, &hints, &ai)) != 0) {
57            fprintf(stderr, "selectserver: %s\n", gai_strerror(rv));
58            exit(1);
59        }
60
61        for(p = ai; p != NULL; p = p->ai_next) {
62            listener = socket(p->ai_family, p->ai_socktype, p->ai_protocol);
63            if (listener < 0) {
64                continue;
65            }
66
67            // lose the pesky "address already in use" error message
```

```
68          setsockopt(listener, SOL_SOCKET, SO_REUSEADDR, &yes, sizeof(int));
69
70          if (bind(listener, p->ai_addr, p->ai_addrlen) < 0) {
71              close(listener);
72              continue;
73          }
74
75          break;
76      }
77
78      // if we got here, it means we didn't get bound
79      if (p == NULL) {
80          fprintf(stderr, "selectserver: failed to bind\n");
81          exit(2);
82      }
83
84      freeaddrinfo(ai); // all done with this
85
86      // listen
87      if (listen(listener, 10) == -1) {
88          perror("listen");
89          exit(3);
90      }
91
92      // add the listener to the master set
93      FD_SET(listener, &master);
94
95      // keep track of the biggest file descriptor
96      fdmax = listener; // so far, it's this one
97
98      // main loop
99      for(;;) {
100         read_fds = master; // copy it
101         if (select(fdmax+1, &read_fds, NULL, NULL, NULL) == -1) {
102             perror("select");
103             exit(4);
104         }
105
106         // run through the existing connections looking for data to read
107         for(i = 0; i <= fdmax; i++) {
108             if (FD_ISSET(i, &read_fds)) { // we got one!!
109                 if (i == listener) {
110                     // handle new connections
```

```
111              addrlen = sizeof remoteaddr;
112              newfd = accept(listener,
113                  (struct sockaddr *)&remoteaddr,
114                  &addrlen);
115
116              if (newfd == -1) {
117                  perror("accept");
118              } else {
119                  FD_SET(newfd, &master); // add to master set
120                  if (newfd > fdmax) {    // keep track of the max
121                      fdmax = newfd;
122                  }
123                  printf("selectserver: new connection from %s on "
124                      "socket %d\n",
125                      inet_ntop(remoteaddr.ss_family,
126                          get_in_addr((struct sockaddr*)&remoteaddr),
127                          remoteIP, INET6_ADDRSTRLEN),
128                      newfd);
129              }
130          } else {
131              // handle data from a client
132              if ((nbytes = recv(i, buf, sizeof buf, 0)) <= 0) {
133                  // got error or connection closed by client
134                  if (nbytes == 0) {
135                      // connection closed
136                      printf("selectserver: socket %d hung up\n", i);
137                  } else {
138                      perror("recv");
139                  }
140                  close(i); // bye!
141                  FD_CLR(i, &master); // remove from master set
142              } else {
143                  // we got some data from a client
144                  for(j = 0; j <= fdmax; j++) {
145                      // send to everyone!
146                      if (FD_ISSET(j, &master)) {
147                          // except the listener and ourselves
148                          if (j != listener && j != i) {
149                              if (send(j, buf, nbytes, 0) == -1) {
150                                  perror("send");
151                              }
152                          }
153                      }
```

```
154                              }
155                         }
156                    } // END handle data from client
157                } // END got new incoming connection
158            } // END looping through file descriptors
159        } // END for(;;)--and you thought it would never end!
160
161        return 0;
162    }
```

Notice I have two file descriptor sets in the code: `master` and `read_fds`. The first, `master`, holds all the socket descriptors that are currently connected, as well as the socket descriptor that is listening for new connections.

The reason I have the `master` set is that `select()` actually *changes* the set you pass into it to reflect which sockets are ready to read. Since I have to keep track of the connections from one call of `select()` to the next, I must store these safely away somewhere. At the last minute, I copy the `master` into the `read_fds`, and then call `select()`.

But doesn't this mean that every time I get a new connection, I have to add it to the `master` set? Yup! And every time a connection closes, I have to remove it from the `master` set? Yes, it does.

Notice I check to see when the `listener` socket is ready to read. When it is, it means I have a new connection pending, and I `accept()` it and add it to the `master` set. Similarly, when a client connection is ready to read, and `recv()` returns 0, I know the client has closed the connection, and I must remove it from the `master` set.

If the client `recv()` returns non-zero, though, I know some data has been received. So I get it, and then go through the `master` list and send that data to all the rest of the connected clients.

And that, my friends, is a less-than-simple overview of the almighty `select()` function.

Quick note to all you Linux fans out there: sometimes, in rare circumstances, Linux's `select()` can return "ready-to-read" and then not actually be ready to read! This means it will block on the `read()` after the `select()` says it won't! Why you little—! Anyway, the workaround solution is to set the `O_NONBLOCK` flag on the receiving socket so it errors with `EWOULDBLOCK` (which you can just safely ignore if it occurs). See the `fcntl()` reference page for more info on setting a socket to non-blocking.

In addition, here is a bonus afterthought: there is another function called `poll()` which behaves much the same way `select()` does, but with a different system for managing the file descriptor sets. Check it out!

Handling Partial send()s

Remember back in the section about send(), above, when I said that send() might not send all the bytes you asked it to? That is, you want it to send 512 bytes, but it returns 412. What happened to the remaining 100 bytes?

Well, they're still in your little buffer waiting to be sent out. Due to circumstances beyond your control, the kernel decided not to send all the data out in one chunk, and now, my friend, it's up to you to get the data out there.

You could write a function like this to do it, too:

```
1    #include <sys/types.h>
2    #include <sys/socket.h>
3
4    int sendall(int s, char *buf, int *len)
5    {
6        int total = 0;        // how many bytes we've sent
7        int bytesleft = *len; // how many we have left to send
8        int n;
9
10       while(total < *len) {
11           n = send(s, buf+total, bytesleft, 0);
12           if (n == -1) { break; }
13           total += n;
14           bytesleft -= n;
15       }
16
17       *len = total; // return number actually sent here
18
19       return n==-1?-1:0; // return -1 on failure, 0 on success
20   }
```

In this example, s is the socket you want to send the data to, buf is the buffer containing the data, and len is a pointer to an int containing the number of bytes in the buffer.

The function returns -1 on error (and errno is still set from the call to send()). Also, the number of bytes actually sent is returned in len. This will be the same number of bytes you asked it to send, unless there was an error. sendall() will do it's best, huffing and puffing, to send the data out, but if there's an error, it gets back to you right away.

For completeness, here's a sample call to the function:

```
1    char buf[10] = "Beej!";
2    int len;
3
4    len = strlen(buf);
```

```
5  if (sendall(s, buf, &len) == -1) {
6      perror("sendall");
7      printf("We only sent %d bytes because of the error!\n", len);
8  }
```

What happens on the receiver's end when part of a packet arrives? If the packets are variable length, how does the receiver know when one packet ends and another begins? Yes, real-world scenarios are a royal pain in the donkeys. You probably have to *encapsulate* (remember that from the data encapsulation section way back there at the beginning?) Read on for details!

Serialization—How to Pack Data

It's easy enough to send text data across the network, you're finding, but what happens if you want to send some "binary" data like ints or floats? It turns out you have a few options.

1. Convert the number into text with a function like sprintf(), then send the text. The receiver will parse the text back into a number using a function like strtol().

2. Just send the data raw, passing a pointer to the data to send().

3. Encode the number into a portable binary form. The receiver will decode it.

Sneak preview! Tonight only!

[*Curtain raises*]

Beej says, "I prefer Method Three, above!"

[*THE END*]

(Before I begin this section in earnest, I should tell you that there are libraries out there for doing this, and rolling your own and remaining portable and error-free is quite a challenge. So hunt around and do your homework before deciding to implement this stuff yourself. I include the information here for those curious about how things like this work.)

Actually all the methods, above, have their drawbacks and advantages, but, like I said, in general, I prefer the third method. First, though, let's talk about some of the drawbacks and advantages to the other two.

The first method, encoding the numbers as text before sending, has the advantage that you can easily print and read the data that's coming over the wire. Sometimes a human-readable protocol is excellent to use in a non-bandwidth-intensive situation, such as with Internet Relay Chat (IRC)[33]. However, it has the disadvantage that it is slow to convert, and the results almost always take up more space than the original number!

---

[33]https://en.wikipedia.org/wiki/Internet_Relay_Chat

Method two: passing the raw data. This one is quite easy (but dangerous!): just take a pointer to the data to send, and call send with it.

```
double d = 3490.15926535;

send(s, &d, sizeof d, 0);   /* DANGER--non-portable! */
```

The receiver gets it like this:

```
double d;

recv(s, &d, sizeof d, 0);   /* DANGER--non-portable! */
```

Fast, simple—what's not to like? Well, it turns out that not all architectures represent a double (or int for that matter) with the same bit representation or even the same byte ordering! The code is decidedly non-portable. (Hey—maybe you don't need portability, in which case this is nice and fast.)

When packing integer types, we've already seen how the htons()-class of functions can help keep things portable by transforming the numbers into Network Byte Order, and how that's the Right Thing to do. Unfortunately, there are no similar functions for float types. Is all hope lost?

Fear not! (Were you afraid there for a second? No? Not even a little bit?) There is something we can do: we can pack (or "marshal", or "serialize", or one of a thousand million other names) the data into a known binary format that the receiver can unpack on the remote side.

What do I mean by "known binary format"? Well, we've already seen the htons() example, right? It changes (or "encodes", if you want to think of it that way) a number from whatever the host format is into Network Byte Order. To reverse (unencode) the number, the receiver calls ntohs().

But didn't I just get finished saying there wasn't any such function for other non-integer types? Yes. I did. And since there's no standard way in C to do this, it's a bit of a pickle (that a gratuitous pun there for you Python fans).

The thing to do is to pack the data into a known format and send that over the wire for decoding. For example, to pack floats, here's something quick and dirty with plenty of room for improvement[34]:

```
1  #include <stdint.h>
2
3  uint32_t htonf(float f)
4  {
5      uint32_t p;
6      uint32_t sign;
```

---

[34]https://beej.us/guide/bgnet/examples/pack.c

```
7
8      if (f < 0) { sign = 1; f = -f; }
9      else { sign = 0; }
10
11     p = ((((uint32_t)f)&0x7fff)<<16) | (sign<<31); // whole part and sign
12     p |= (uint32_t)(((f - (int)f) * 65536.0f))&0xffff; // fraction
13
14     return p;
15  }
16
17  float ntohf(uint32_t p)
18  {
19      float f = ((p>>16)&0x7fff); // whole part
20      f += (p&0xffff) / 65536.0f; // fraction
21
22      if (((p>>31)&0x1) == 0x1) { f = -f; } // sign bit set
23
24      return f;
25  }
```

The above code is sort of a naive implementation that stores a `float` in a 32-bit number. The high bit (31) is used to store the sign of the number ("1" means negative), and the next seven bits (30-16) are used to store the whole number portion of the `float`. Finally, the remaining bits (15-0) are used to store the fractional portion of the number.

Usage is fairly straightforward:

```
1   #include <stdio.h>
2
3   int main(void)
4   {
5       float f = 3.1415926, f2;
6       uint32_t netf;
7
8       netf = htonf(f);   // convert to "network" form
9       f2 = ntohf(netf);  // convert back to test
10
11      printf("Original: %f\n", f);          // 3.141593
12      printf(" Network: 0x%08X\n", netf);   // 0x0003243F
13      printf("Unpacked: %f\n", f2);         // 3.141586
14
15      return 0;
16  }
```

On the plus side, it's small, simple, and fast. On the minus side, it's not an efficient use of space and the range is severely restricted—try storing a number greater-than 32767 in there and it won't be very happy! You can also see in the above example that the last couple decimal places are not correctly preserved.

What can we do instead? Well, *The* Standard for storing floating point numbers is known as IEEE-754[35]. Most computers use this format internally for doing floating point math, so in those cases, strictly speaking, conversion wouldn't need to be done. But if you want your source code to be portable, that's an assumption you can't necessarily make. (On the other hand, if you want things to be fast, you should optimize this out on platforms that don't need to do it! That's what `htons()` and its ilk do.)

Here's some code that encodes floats and doubles into IEEE-754 format[36]. (Mostly—it doesn't encode NaN or Infinity, but it could be modified to do that.)

```
1   #define pack754_32(f) (pack754((f), 32, 8))
2   #define pack754_64(f) (pack754((f), 64, 11))
3   #define unpack754_32(i) (unpack754((i), 32, 8))
4   #define unpack754_64(i) (unpack754((i), 64, 11))
5
6   uint64_t pack754(long double f, unsigned bits, unsigned expbits)
7   {
8       long double fnorm;
9       int shift;
10      long long sign, exp, significand;
11      unsigned significandbits = bits - expbits - 1; // -1 for sign bit
12
13      if (f == 0.0) return 0; // get this special case out of the way
14
15      // check sign and begin normalization
16      if (f < 0) { sign = 1; fnorm = -f; }
17      else { sign = 0; fnorm = f; }
18
19      // get the normalized form of f and track the exponent
20      shift = 0;
21      while(fnorm >= 2.0) { fnorm /= 2.0; shift++; }
22      while(fnorm < 1.0) { fnorm *= 2.0; shift--; }
23      fnorm = fnorm - 1.0;
24
25      // calculate the binary form (non-float) of the significand data
26      significand = fnorm * ((1LL<<significandbits) + 0.5f);
27
28      // get the biased exponent
29      exp = shift + ((1<<(expbits-1)) - 1); // shift + bias
```

[35]https://en.wikipedia.org/wiki/IEEE_754
[36]https://beej.us/guide/bgnet/examples/ieee754.c

```
30
31      // return the final answer
32      return (sign<<(bits-1)) | (exp<<(bits-expbits-1)) | significand;
33  }
34
35  long double unpack754(uint64_t i, unsigned bits, unsigned expbits)
36  {
37      long double result;
38      long long shift;
39      unsigned bias;
40      unsigned significandbits = bits - expbits - 1; // -1 for sign bit
41
42      if (i == 0) return 0.0;
43
44      // pull the significand
45      result = (i&((1LL<<significandbits)-1)); // mask
46      result /= (1LL<<significandbits); // convert back to float
47      result += 1.0f; // add the one back on
48
49      // deal with the exponent
50      bias = (1<<(expbits-1)) - 1;
51      shift = ((i>>significandbits)&((1LL<<expbits)-1)) - bias;
52      while(shift > 0) { result *= 2.0; shift--; }
53      while(shift < 0) { result /= 2.0; shift++; }
54
55      // sign it
56      result *= (i>>(bits-1))&1? -1.0: 1.0;
57
58      return result;
59  }
```

I put some handy macros up there at the top for packing and unpacking 32-bit (probably a float) and 64-bit (probably a double) numbers, but the pack754() function could be called directly and told to encode bits-worth of data (expbits of which are reserved for the normalized number's exponent).

Here's sample usage:

```
1
2   #include <stdio.h>
3   #include <stdint.h> // defines uintN_t types
4   #include <inttypes.h> // defines PRIx macros
5
6   int main(void)
7   {
```

```
8      float f = 3.1415926, f2;
9      double d = 3.14159265358979323, d2;
10     uint32_t fi;
11     uint64_t di;
12
13     fi = pack754_32(f);
14     f2 = unpack754_32(fi);
15
16     di = pack754_64(d);
17     d2 = unpack754_64(di);
18
19     printf("float before : %.7f\n", f);
20     printf("float encoded: 0x%08" PRIx32 "\n", fi);
21     printf("float after  : %.7f\n\n", f2);
22
23     printf("double before : %.20lf\n", d);
24     printf("double encoded: 0x%016" PRIx64 "\n", di);
25     printf("double after  : %.20lf\n", d2);
26
27     return 0;
28 }
```

The above code produces this output:

```
float before : 3.1415925
float encoded: 0x40490FDA
float after  : 3.1415925

double before : 3.14159265358979311600
double encoded: 0x400921FB54442D18
double after  : 3.14159265358979311600
```

Another question you might have is how do you pack structs? Unfortunately for you, the compiler is free to put padding all over the place in a struct, and that means you can't portably send the whole thing over the wire in one chunk. (Aren't you getting sick of hearing "can't do this", "can't do that"? Sorry! To quote a friend, "Whenever anything goes wrong, I always blame Microsoft." This one might not be Microsoft's fault, admittedly, but my friend's statement is completely true.)

Back to it: the best way to send the struct over the wire is to pack each field independently and then unpack them into the struct when they arrive on the other side.

That's a lot of work, is what you're thinking. Yes, it is. One thing you can do is write a helper function to help pack the data for you. It'll be fun! Really!

In the book *The Practice of Programming*[37] by Kernighan and Pike, they implement `printf()`-like functions called `pack()` and `unpack()` that do exactly this. I'd link to them, but apparently those functions aren't online with the rest of the source from the book.

(The Practice of Programming is an excellent read. Zeus saves a kitten every time I recommend it.)

At this point, I'm going to drop a pointer to a Protocol Buffers implementation in C[38] which I've never used, but looks completely respectable. Python and Perl programmers will want to check out their language's `pack()` and `unpack()` functions for accomplishing the same thing. And Java has a big-ol' Serializable interface that can be used in a similar way.

But if you want to write your own packing utility in C, K&P's trick is to use variable argument lists to make `printf()`-like functions to build the packets. Here's a version I cooked up[39] on my own based on that which hopefully will be enough to give you an idea of how such a thing can work.

(This code references the `pack754()` functions, above. The `packi*()` functions operate like the familiar `htons()` family, except they pack into a `char` array instead of another integer.)

```c
#include <stdio.h>
#include <ctype.h>
#include <stdarg.h>
#include <string.h>

/*
** packi16() -- store a 16-bit int into a char buffer (like htons())
*/
void packi16(unsigned char *buf, unsigned int i)
{
    *buf++ = i>>8; *buf++ = i;
}

/*
** packi32() -- store a 32-bit int into a char buffer (like htonl())
*/
void packi32(unsigned char *buf, unsigned long int i)
{
    *buf++ = i>>24; *buf++ = i>>16;
    *buf++ = i>>8;  *buf++ = i;
}

```

[37] https://beej.us/guide/url/tpop
[38] https://github.com/protobuf-c/protobuf-c
[39] https://beej.us/guide/bgnet/examples/pack2.c

```
23   /*
24   ** packi64() -- store a 64-bit int into a char buffer (like htonl())
25   */
26   void packi64(unsigned char *buf, unsigned long long int i)
27   {
28       *buf++ = i>>56; *buf++ = i>>48;
29       *buf++ = i>>40; *buf++ = i>>32;
30       *buf++ = i>>24; *buf++ = i>>16;
31       *buf++ = i>>8;  *buf++ = i;
32   }
33
34   /*
35   ** unpacki16() -- unpack a 16-bit int from a char buffer (like ntohs())
36   */
37   int unpacki16(unsigned char *buf)
38   {
39       unsigned int i2 = ((unsigned int)buf[0]<<8) | buf[1];
40       int i;
41
42       // change unsigned numbers to signed
43       if (i2 <= 0x7fffu) { i = i2; }
44       else { i = -1 - (unsigned int)(0xffffu - i2); }
45
46       return i;
47   }
48
49   /*
50   ** unpacku16() -- unpack a 16-bit unsigned from a char buffer (like ntohs())
51   */
52   unsigned int unpacku16(unsigned char *buf)
53   {
54       return ((unsigned int)buf[0]<<8) | buf[1];
55   }
56
57   /*
58   ** unpacki32() -- unpack a 32-bit int from a char buffer (like ntohl())
59   */
60   long int unpacki32(unsigned char *buf)
61   {
62       unsigned long int i2 = ((unsigned long int)buf[0]<<24) |
63                              ((unsigned long int)buf[1]<<16) |
64                              ((unsigned long int)buf[2]<<8)  |
65                              buf[3];
```

```
66      long int i;
67
68      // change unsigned numbers to signed
69      if (i2 <= 0x7fffffffu) { i = i2; }
70      else { i = -1 - (long int)(0xffffffffu - i2); }
71
72      return i;
73  }
74
75  /*
76  ** unpacku32() -- unpack a 32-bit unsigned from a char buffer (like ntohl())
77  */
78  unsigned long int unpacku32(unsigned char *buf)
79  {
80      return ((unsigned long int)buf[0]<<24) |
81             ((unsigned long int)buf[1]<<16) |
82             ((unsigned long int)buf[2]<<8)  |
83             buf[3];
84  }
85
86  /*
87  ** unpacki64() -- unpack a 64-bit int from a char buffer (like ntohl())
88  */
89  long long int unpacki64(unsigned char *buf)
90  {
91      unsigned long long int i2 = ((unsigned long long int)buf[0]<<56) |
92                                  ((unsigned long long int)buf[1]<<48) |
93                                  ((unsigned long long int)buf[2]<<40) |
94                                  ((unsigned long long int)buf[3]<<32) |
95                                  ((unsigned long long int)buf[4]<<24) |
96                                  ((unsigned long long int)buf[5]<<16) |
97                                  ((unsigned long long int)buf[6]<<8)  |
98                                  buf[7];
99      long long int i;
100
101     // change unsigned numbers to signed
102     if (i2 <= 0x7fffffffffffffffu) { i = i2; }
103     else { i = -1 -(long long int)(0xffffffffffffffffu - i2); }
104
105     return i;
106 }
107
108 /*
```

```
109    ** unpacku64() -- unpack a 64-bit unsigned from a char buffer (like ntohl())
110    */
111    unsigned long long int unpacku64(unsigned char *buf)
112    {
113        return ((unsigned long long int)buf[0]<<56) |
114               ((unsigned long long int)buf[1]<<48) |
115               ((unsigned long long int)buf[2]<<40) |
116               ((unsigned long long int)buf[3]<<32) |
117               ((unsigned long long int)buf[4]<<24) |
118               ((unsigned long long int)buf[5]<<16) |
119               ((unsigned long long int)buf[6]<<8)  |
120               buf[7];
121    }
122
123    /*
124    ** pack() -- store data dictated by the format string in the buffer
125    **
126    **   bits |signed     unsigned     float     string
127    **   -----+--------------------------------------
128    **      8 |   c          C
129    **     16 |   h          H          f
130    **     32 |   l          L          d
131    **     64 |   q          Q          g
132    **      - |                                   s
133    **
134    **   (16-bit unsigned length is automatically prepended to strings)
135    */
136
137    unsigned int pack(unsigned char *buf, char *format, ...)
138    {
139        va_list ap;
140
141        signed char c;              // 8-bit
142        unsigned char C;
143
144        int h;                      // 16-bit
145        unsigned int H;
146
147        long int l;                 // 32-bit
148        unsigned long int L;
149
150        long long int q;            // 64-bit
151        unsigned long long int Q;
```

```
152
153     float f;                        // floats
154     double d;
155     long double g;
156     unsigned long long int fhold;
157
158     char *s;                        // strings
159     unsigned int len;
160
161     unsigned int size = 0;
162
163     va_start(ap, format);
164
165     for(; *format != '\0'; format++) {
166         switch(*format) {
167         case 'c': // 8-bit
168             size += 1;
169             c = (signed char)va_arg(ap, int); // promoted
170             *buf++ = c;
171             break;
172
173         case 'C': // 8-bit unsigned
174             size += 1;
175             C = (unsigned char)va_arg(ap, unsigned int); // promoted
176             *buf++ = C;
177             break;
178
179         case 'h': // 16-bit
180             size += 2;
181             h = va_arg(ap, int);
182             packi16(buf, h);
183             buf += 2;
184             break;
185
186         case 'H': // 16-bit unsigned
187             size += 2;
188             H = va_arg(ap, unsigned int);
189             packi16(buf, H);
190             buf += 2;
191             break;
192
193         case 'l': // 32-bit
194             size += 4;
```

```
195             l = va_arg(ap, long int);
196             packi32(buf, l);
197             buf += 4;
198             break;
199
200         case 'L': // 32-bit unsigned
201             size += 4;
202             L = va_arg(ap, unsigned long int);
203             packi32(buf, L);
204             buf += 4;
205             break;
206
207         case 'q': // 64-bit
208             size += 8;
209             q = va_arg(ap, long long int);
210             packi64(buf, q);
211             buf += 8;
212             break;
213
214         case 'Q': // 64-bit unsigned
215             size += 8;
216             Q = va_arg(ap, unsigned long long int);
217             packi64(buf, Q);
218             buf += 8;
219             break;
220
221         case 'f': // float-16
222             size += 2;
223             f = (float)va_arg(ap, double); // promoted
224             fhold = pack754_16(f); // convert to IEEE 754
225             packi16(buf, fhold);
226             buf += 2;
227             break;
228
229         case 'd': // float-32
230             size += 4;
231             d = va_arg(ap, double);
232             fhold = pack754_32(d); // convert to IEEE 754
233             packi32(buf, fhold);
234             buf += 4;
235             break;
236
237         case 'g': // float-64
```

```
238              size += 8;
239              g = va_arg(ap, long double);
240              fhold = pack754_64(g); // convert to IEEE 754
241              packi64(buf, fhold);
242              buf += 8;
243              break;
244
245          case 's': // string
246              s = va_arg(ap, char*);
247              len = strlen(s);
248              size += len + 2;
249              packi16(buf, len);
250              buf += 2;
251              memcpy(buf, s, len);
252              buf += len;
253              break;
254          }
255      }
256
257      va_end(ap);
258
259      return size;
260  }
261
262  /*
263  ** unpack() -- unpack data dictated by the format string into the buffer
264  **
265  **   bits |signed    unsigned    float    string
266  **   -----+----------------------------------------
267  **      8 |  c          C
268  **     16 |  h          H          f
269  **     32 |  l          L          d
270  **     64 |  q          Q          g
271  **      - |                                   s
272  **
273  ** (string is extracted based on its stored length, but 's' can be
274  ** prepended with a max length)
275  */
276  void unpack(unsigned char *buf, char *format, ...)
277  {
278      va_list ap;
279
280      signed char *c;                 // 8-bit
```

```
281        unsigned char *C;
282
283        int *h;                          // 16-bit
284        unsigned int *H;
285
286        long int *l;                     // 32-bit
287        unsigned long int *L;
288
289        long long int *q;                // 64-bit
290        unsigned long long int *Q;
291
292        float *f;                        // floats
293        double *d;
294        long double *g;
295        unsigned long long int fhold;
296
297        char *s;
298        unsigned int len, maxstrlen=0, count;
299
300        va_start(ap, format);
301
302        for(; *format != '\0'; format++) {
303            switch(*format) {
304            case 'c': // 8-bit
305                c = va_arg(ap, signed char*);
306                if (*buf <= 0x7f) { *c = *buf;} // re-sign
307                else { *c = -1 - (unsigned char)(0xffu - *buf); }
308                buf++;
309                break;
310
311            case 'C': // 8-bit unsigned
312                C = va_arg(ap, unsigned char*);
313                *C = *buf++;
314                break;
315
316            case 'h': // 16-bit
317                h = va_arg(ap, int*);
318                *h = unpacki16(buf);
319                buf += 2;
320                break;
321
322            case 'H': // 16-bit unsigned
323                H = va_arg(ap, unsigned int*);
```

```
324          *H = unpacku16(buf);
325          buf += 2;
326          break;
327
328      case 'l': // 32-bit
329          l = va_arg(ap, long int*);
330          *l = unpacki32(buf);
331          buf += 4;
332          break;
333
334      case 'L': // 32-bit unsigned
335          L = va_arg(ap, unsigned long int*);
336          *L = unpacku32(buf);
337          buf += 4;
338          break;
339
340      case 'q': // 64-bit
341          q = va_arg(ap, long long int*);
342          *q = unpacki64(buf);
343          buf += 8;
344          break;
345
346      case 'Q': // 64-bit unsigned
347          Q = va_arg(ap, unsigned long long int*);
348          *Q = unpacku64(buf);
349          buf += 8;
350          break;
351
352      case 'f': // float
353          f = va_arg(ap, float*);
354          fhold = unpacku16(buf);
355          *f = unpack754_16(fhold);
356          buf += 2;
357          break;
358
359      case 'd': // float-32
360          d = va_arg(ap, double*);
361          fhold = unpacku32(buf);
362          *d = unpack754_32(fhold);
363          buf += 4;
364          break;
365
366      case 'g': // float-64
```

```
367        g = va_arg(ap, long double*);
368        fhold = unpacku64(buf);
369        *g = unpack754_64(fhold);
370        buf += 8;
371        break;
372
373    case 's': // string
374        s = va_arg(ap, char*);
375        len = unpacku16(buf);
376        buf += 2;
377        if (maxstrlen > 0 && len >= maxstrlen) count = maxstrlen - 1;
378        else count = len;
379        memcpy(s, buf, count);
380        s[count] = '\0';
381        buf += len;
382        break;
383
384    default:
385        if (isdigit(*format)) { // track max str len
386            maxstrlen = maxstrlen * 10 + (*format-'0');
387        }
388    }
389
390    if (!isdigit(*format)) maxstrlen = 0;
391    }
392
393    va_end(ap);
394 }
```

And here is a demonstration program[40] of the above code that packs some data into `buf` and then unpacks it into variables. Note that when calling `unpack()` with a string argument (format specifier "s"), it's wise to put a maximum length count in front of it to prevent a buffer overrun, e.g. "96s". Be wary when unpacking data you get over the network—a malicious user might send badly-constructed packets in an effort to attack your system!

```
1  #include <stdio.h>
2
3  // various bits for floating point types--
4  // varies for different architectures
5  typedef float float32_t;
6  typedef double float64_t;
7
8  int main(void)
```

---

[40]https://beej.us/guide/bgnet/examples/pack2.c

```
9    {
10       unsigned char buf[1024];
11       int8_t magic;
12       int16_t monkeycount;
13       int32_t altitude;
14       float32_t absurdityfactor;
15       char *s = "Great unmitigated Zot! You've found the Runestaff!";
16       char s2[96];
17       int16_t packetsize, ps2;
18
19       packetsize = pack(buf, "chhlsf", (int8_t)'B', (int16_t)0, (int16_t)37,
20              (int32_t)-5, s, (float32_t)-3490.6677);
21       packi16(buf+1, packetsize); // store packet size in packet for kicks
22
23       printf("packet is %" PRId32 " bytes\n", packetsize);
24
25       unpack(buf, "chhl96sf", &magic, &ps2, &monkeycount, &altitude, s2,
26              &absurdityfactor);
27
28       printf("'%c' %" PRId32" %" PRId16 " %" PRId32
29              " \"%s\" %f\n", magic, ps2, monkeycount,
30              altitude, s2, absurdityfactor);
31
32       return 0;
33    }
```

Whether you roll your own code or use someone else's, it's a good idea to have a general set of data packing routines for the sake of keeping bugs in check, rather than packing each bit by hand each time.

When packing the data, what's a good format to use? Excellent question. Fortunately, RFC 4506[41], the External Data Representation Standard, already defines binary formats for a bunch of different types, like floating point types, integer types, arrays, raw data, etc. I suggest conforming to that if you're going to roll the data yourself. But you're not obligated to. The Packet Police are not right outside your door. At least, I don't *think* they are.

In any case, encoding the data somehow or another before you send it is the right way of doing things!

Son of Data Encapsulation

What does it really mean to encapsulate data, anyway? In the simplest case, it means you'll stick a header on there with either some identifying information or a packet length, or both.

---

[41] https://tools.ietf.org/html/rfc4506

What should your header look like? Well, it's just some binary data that represents whatever you feel is necessary to complete your project.

Wow. That's vague.

Okay. For instance, let's say you have a multi-user chat program that uses SOCK_STREAMs. When a user types ("says") something, two pieces of information need to be transmitted to the server: what was said and who said it.

So far so good? "What's the problem?" you're asking.

The problem is that the messages can be of varying lengths. One person named "tom" might say, "Hi", and another person named "Benjamin" might say, "Hey guys what is up?"

So you send() all this stuff to the clients as it comes in. Your outgoing data stream looks like this:

```
    t o m H i B e n j a m i n H e y g u y s w h a t i s u p ?
```

And so on. How does the client know when one message starts and another stops? You could, if you wanted, make all messages the same length and just call the sendall() we implemented, above. But that wastes bandwidth! We don't want to send() 1024 bytes just so "tom" can say "Hi".

So we *encapsulate* the data in a tiny header and packet structure. Both the client and server know how to pack and unpack (sometimes referred to as "marshal" and "unmarshal") this data. Don't look now, but we're starting to define a *protocol* that describes how a client and server communicate!

In this case, let's assume the user name is a fixed length of 8 characters, padded with '\0'. And then let's assume the data is variable length, up to a maximum of 128 characters. Let's have a look a sample packet structure that we might use in this situation:

1. len (1 byte, unsigned)—The total length of the packet, counting the 8-byte user name and chat data.

2. name (8 bytes)—The user's name, NUL-padded if necessary.

3. chatdata (*n*-bytes)—The data itself, no more than 128 bytes. The length of the packet should be calculated as the length of this data plus 8 (the length of the name field, above).

Why did I choose the 8-byte and 128-byte limits for the fields? I pulled them out of the air, assuming they'd be long enough. Maybe, though, 8 bytes is too restrictive for your needs, and you can have a 30-byte name field, or whatever. The choice is up to you.

Using the above packet definition, the first packet would consist of the following information (in hex and ASCII):

```
     0A      74 6F 6D 00 00 00 00 00      48 69
  (length)   T  o  m    (padding)         H  i
```

And the second is similar:

```
   18      42 65 6E 6A 61 6D 69 6E      48 65 79 20 67 75 79 73 20 77 ...
(length)   B  e  n  j  a  m  i  n       H  e  y     g  u  y  s     w  ...
```

(The length is stored in Network Byte Order, of course. In this case, it's only one byte so it doesn't matter, but generally speaking you'll want all your binary integers to be stored in Network Byte Order in your packets.)

When you're sending this data, you should be safe and use a command similar to `sendall()`, above, so you know all the data is sent, even if it takes multiple calls to `send()` to get it all out.

Likewise, when you're receiving this data, you need to do a bit of extra work. To be safe, you should assume that you might receive a partial packet (like maybe we receive "18 42 65 6E 6A" from Benjamin, above, but that's all we get in this call to `recv()`). We need to call `recv()` over and over again until the packet is completely received.

But how? Well, we know the number of bytes we need to receive in total for the packet to be complete, since that number is tacked on the front of the packet. We also know the maximum packet size is 1+8+128, or 137 bytes (because that's how we defined the packet).

There are actually a couple things you can do here. Since you know every packet starts off with a length, you can call `recv()` just to get the packet length. Then once you have that, you can call it again specifying exactly the remaining length of the packet (possibly repeatedly to get all the data) until you have the complete packet. The advantage of this method is that you only need a buffer large enough for one packet, while the disadvantage is that you need to call `recv()` at least twice to get all the data.

Another option is just to call `recv()` and say the amount you're willing to receive is the maximum number of bytes in a packet. Then whatever you get, stick it onto the back of a buffer, and finally check to see if the packet is complete. Of course, you might get some of the next packet, so you'll need to have room for that.

What you can do is declare an array big enough for two packets. This is your work array where you will reconstruct packets as they arrive.

Every time you `recv()` data, you'll append it into the work buffer and check to see if the packet is complete. That is, the number of bytes in the buffer is greater than or equal to the length specified in the header (+1, because the length in the header doesn't include the byte for the length itself). If the number of bytes in the buffer is less than 1, the packet is not complete, obviously. You have to make a special case for this, though, since the first byte is garbage and you can't rely on it for the correct packet length.

Once the packet is complete, you can do with it what you will. Use it, and remove it from your work buffer.

Whew! Are you juggling that in your head yet? Well, here's the second of the one-two punch: you might have read past the end of one packet and onto the next in a single `recv()`

call. That is, you have a work buffer with one complete packet, and an incomplete part of the next packet! Bloody heck. (But this is why you made your work buffer large enough to hold *two* packets—in case this happened!)

Since you know the length of the first packet from the header, and you've been keeping track of the number of bytes in the work buffer, you can subtract and calculate how many of the bytes in the work buffer belong to the second (incomplete) packet. When you've handled the first one, you can clear it out of the work buffer and move the partial second packet down the to front of the buffer so it's all ready to go for the next recv( ).

(Some of you readers will note that actually moving the partial second packet to the beginning of the work buffer takes time, and the program can be coded to not require this by using a circular buffer. Unfortunately for the rest of you, a discussion on circular buffers is beyond the scope of this article. If you're still curious, grab a data structures book and go from there.)

I never said it was easy. Ok, I did say it was easy. And it is; you just need practice and pretty soon it'll come to you naturally. By Excalibur I swear it!

Broadcast Packets—Hello, World!

So far, this guide has talked about sending data from one host to one other host. But it is possible, I insist, that you can, with the proper authority, send data to multiple hosts *at the same time*!

With UDP (only UDP, not TCP) and standard IPv4, this is done through a mechanism called *broadcasting*. With IPv6, broadcasting isn't supported, and you have to resort to the often superior technique of *multicasting*, which, sadly I won't be discussing at this time. But enough of the starry-eyed future—we're stuck in the 32-bit present.

But wait! You can't just run off and start broadcasting willy-nilly; You have to set the socket option SO_BROADCAST before you can send a broadcast packet out on the network. It's like a one of those little plastic covers they put over the missile launch switch! That's just how much power you hold in your hands!

But seriously, though, there is a danger to using broadcast packets, and that is: every system that receives a broadcast packet must undo all the onion-skin layers of data encapsulation until it finds out what port the data is destined to. And then it hands the data over or discards it. In either case, it's a lot of work for each machine that receives the broadcast packet, and since it is all of them on the local network, that could be a lot of machines doing a lot of unnecessary work. When the game Doom first came out, this was a complaint about its network code.

Now, there is more than one way to skin a cat... wait a minute. Is there really more than one way to skin a cat? What kind of expression is that? Uh, and likewise, there is more than one way to send a broadcast packet. So, to get to the meat and potatoes of the whole thing: how do you specify the destination address for a broadcast message? There are two common ways:

1. Send the data to a specific subnet's broadcast address. This is the subnet's network number with all one-bits set for the host portion of the address. For instance, at home my network is `192.168.1.0`, my netmask is `255.255.255.0`, so the last byte of the address is my host number (because the first three bytes, according to the netmask, are the network number). So my broadcast address is `192.168.1.255`. Under Unix, the `ifconfig` command will actually give you all this data. (If you're curious, the bitwise logic to get your broadcast address is `network_number` OR (NOT `netmask`).) You can send this type of broadcast packet to remote networks as well as your local network, but you run the risk of the packet being dropped by the destination's router. (If they didn't drop it, then some random smurf could start flooding their LAN with broadcast traffic.)

2. Send the data to the "global" broadcast address. This is `255.255.255.255`, aka `INADDR_BROADCAST`. Many machines will automatically bitwise AND this with your network number to convert it to a network broadcast address, but some won't. It varies. Routers do not forward this type of broadcast packet off your local network, ironically enough.

So what happens if you try to send data on the broadcast address without first setting the `SO_BROADCAST` socket option? Well, let's fire up good old `talker` and `listener` and see what happens.

```
$ talker 192.168.1.2 foo
sent 3 bytes to 192.168.1.2
$ talker 192.168.1.255 foo
sendto: Permission denied
$ talker 255.255.255.255 foo
sendto: Permission denied
```

Yes, it's not happy at all...because we didn't set the `SO_BROADCAST` socket option. Do that, and now you can `sendto()` anywhere you want!

In fact, that's the *only difference* between a UDP application that can broadcast and one that can't. So let's take the old `talker` application and add one section that sets the `SO_BROADCAST` socket option. We'll call this program `broadcaster.c`[42]:

```
1   /*
2   ** broadcaster.c -- a datagram "client" like talker.c, except
3   **                  this one can broadcast
4   */
5
6   #include <stdio.h>
```

---
[42]https://beej.us/guide/bgnet/examples/broadcaster.c

```
 7  #include <stdlib.h>
 8  #include <unistd.h>
 9  #include <errno.h>
10  #include <string.h>
11  #include <sys/types.h>
12  #include <sys/socket.h>
13  #include <netinet/in.h>
14  #include <arpa/inet.h>
15  #include <netdb.h>
16
17  #define SERVERPORT 4950 // the port users will be connecting to
18
19  int main(int argc, char *argv[])
20  {
21      int sockfd;
22      struct sockaddr_in their_addr; // connector's address information
23      struct hostent *he;
24      int numbytes;
25      int broadcast = 1;
26      //char broadcast = '1'; // if that doesn't work, try this
27
28      if (argc != 3) {
29          fprintf(stderr,"usage: broadcaster hostname message\n");
30          exit(1);
31      }
32
33      if ((he=gethostbyname(argv[1])) == NULL) {  // get the host info
34          perror("gethostbyname");
35          exit(1);
36      }
37
38      if ((sockfd = socket(AF_INET, SOCK_DGRAM, 0)) == -1) {
39          perror("socket");
40          exit(1);
41      }
42
43      // this call is what allows broadcast packets to be sent:
44      if (setsockopt(sockfd, SOL_SOCKET, SO_BROADCAST, &broadcast,
45          sizeof broadcast) == -1) {
46          perror("setsockopt (SO_BROADCAST)");
47          exit(1);
48      }
49
```

```
50    their_addr.sin_family = AF_INET;      // host byte order
51    their_addr.sin_port = htons(SERVERPORT); // short, network byte order
52    their_addr.sin_addr = *((struct in_addr *)he->h_addr);
53    memset(their_addr.sin_zero, '\0', sizeof their_addr.sin_zero);
54
55    if ((numbytes=sendto(sockfd, argv[2], strlen(argv[2]), 0,
56            (struct sockaddr *)&their_addr, sizeof their_addr)) == -1) {
57        perror("sendto");
58        exit(1);
59    }
60
61    printf("sent %d bytes to %s\n", numbytes,
62        inet_ntoa(their_addr.sin_addr));
63
64    close(sockfd);
65
66    return 0;
67 }
```

What's different between this and a "normal" UDP client/server situation? Nothing! (With the exception of the client being allowed to send broadcast packets in this case.) As such, go ahead and run the old UDP listener program in one window, and broadcaster in another. You should be now be able to do all those sends that failed, above.

```
$ broadcaster 192.168.1.2 foo
sent 3 bytes to 192.168.1.2
$ broadcaster 192.168.1.255 foo
sent 3 bytes to 192.168.1.255
$ broadcaster 255.255.255.255 foo
sent 3 bytes to 255.255.255.255
```

And you should see listener responding that it got the packets. (If listener doesn't respond, it could be because it's bound to an IPv6 address. Try changing the AF_UNSPEC in listener.c to AF_INET to force IPv4.)

Well, that's kind of exciting. But now fire up listener on another machine next to you on the same network so that you have two copies going, one on each machine, and run broadcaster again with your broadcast address... Hey! Both listeners get the packet even though you only called sendto() once! Cool!

If the listener gets data you send directly to it, but not data on the broadcast address, it could be that you have a firewall on your local machine that is blocking the packets. (Yes, Pat and Bapper, thank you for realizing before I did that this is why my sample code wasn't working. I told you I'd mention you in the guide, and here you are. So *nyah*.)

Again, be careful with broadcast packets. Since every machine on the LAN will be forced to deal with the packet whether it `recvfrom()`s it or not, it can present quite a load to the entire computing network. They are definitely to be used sparingly and appropriately.

Common Questions

Where can I get those header files?

If you don't have them on your system already, you probably don't need them. Check the manual for your particular platform. If you're building for Windows, you only need to #include <winsock.h>.

What do I do when bind() reports "Address already in use"?

You have to use setsockopt() with the SO_REUSEADDR option on the listening socket. Check out the section on bind() and the section on select() for an example.

How do I get a list of open sockets on the system?

Use the netstat. Check the man page for full details, but you should get some good output just typing:

```
$ netstat
```

The only trick is determining which socket is associated with which program. :-)

How can I view the routing table?

Run the route command (in /sbin on most Linuxes) or the command netstat -r.

How can I run the client and server programs if I only have one computer? Don't I need a network to write network programs?

Fortunately for you, virtually all machines implement a loopback network "device" that sits in the kernel and pretends to be a network card. (This is the interface listed as "lo" in the routing table.)

Pretend you're logged into a machine named "goat". Run the client in one window and the server in another. Or start the server in the background ("server &") and run the client in the same window. The upshot of the loopback device is that you can either client goat or client localhost (since "localhost" is likely defined in your /etc/hosts file) and you'll have the client talking to the server without a network!

In short, no changes are necessary to any of the code to make it run on a single non-networked machine! Huzzah!

How can I tell if the remote side has closed connection?

You can tell because `recv()` will return 0.

How do I implement a "ping" utility? What is ICMP? Where can I find out more about raw sockets and SOCK_RAW?

All your raw sockets questions will be answered in W. Richard Stevens' UNIX Network Programming books. Also, look in the `ping/` subdirectory in Stevens' UNIX Network Programming source code, available online[43].

How do I change or shorten the timeout on a call to `connect()`?

Instead of giving you exactly the same answer that W. Richard Stevens would give you, I'll just refer you to `lib/connect_nonb.c` in the UNIX Network Programming source code[44].

The gist of it is that you make a socket descriptor with `socket()`, set it to non-blocking, call `connect()`, and if all goes well `connect()` will return -1 immediately and `errno` will be set to `EINPROGRESS`. Then you call `select()` with whatever timeout you want, passing the socket descriptor in both the read and write sets. If it doesn't timeout, it means the `connect()` call completed. At this point, you'll have to use `getsockopt()` with the `SO_ERROR` option to get the return value from the `connect()` call, which should be zero if there was no error.

Finally, you'll probably want to set the socket back to be blocking again before you start transferring data over it.

Notice that this has the added benefit of allowing your program to do something else while it's connecting, too. You could, for example, set the timeout to something low, like 500 ms, and update an indicator onscreen each timeout, then call `select()` again. When you've called `select()` and timed-out, say, 20 times, you'll know it's time to give up on the connection.

Like I said, check out Stevens' source for a perfectly excellent example.

How do I build for Windows?

First, delete Windows and install Linux or BSD. };-). No, actually, just see the section on building for Windows in the introduction.

How do I build for Solaris/SunOS? I keep getting linker errors when I try to compile!

The linker errors happen because Sun boxes don't automatically compile in the socket libraries. See the section on building for Solaris/SunOS in the introduction for an example of how to do this.

---

[43]http://www.unpbook.com/src.html
[44]http://www.unpbook.com/src.html

Why does `select()` keep falling out on a signal?

Signals tend to cause blocked system calls to return `-1` with `errno` set to `EINTR`. When you set up a signal handler with `sigaction()`, you can set the flag `SA_RESTART`, which is supposed to restart the system call after it was interrupted.

Naturally, this doesn't always work.

My favorite solution to this involves a `goto` statement. You know this irritates your professors to no end, so go for it!

```
select_restart:
if ((err = select(fdmax+1, &readfds, NULL, NULL, NULL)) == -1) {
    if (errno == EINTR) {
        // some signal just interrupted us, so restart
        goto select_restart;
    }
    // handle the real error here:
    perror("select");
}
```

Sure, you don't *need* to use `goto` in this case; you can use other structures to control it. But I think the `goto` statement is actually cleaner.

How can I implement a timeout on a call to `recv()`?

Use `select()`! It allows you to specify a timeout parameter for socket descriptors that you're looking to read from. Or, you could wrap the entire functionality in a single function, like this:

```
#include <unistd.h>
#include <sys/time.h>
#include <sys/types.h>
#include <sys/socket.h>

int recvtimeout(int s, char *buf, int len, int timeout)
{
    fd_set fds;
    int n;
    struct timeval tv;

    // set up the file descriptor set
    FD_ZERO(&fds);
    FD_SET(s, &fds);

    // set up the struct timeval for the timeout
    tv.tv_sec = timeout;
```

```
18      tv.tv_usec = 0;
19
20      // wait until timeout or data received
21      n = select(s+1, &fds, NULL, NULL, &tv);
22      if (n == 0) return -2; // timeout!
23      if (n == -1) return -1; // error
24
25      // data must be here, so do a normal recv()
26      return recv(s, buf, len, 0);
27  }
28  .
29  .
30  .
31  // Sample call to recvtimeout():
32  n = recvtimeout(s, buf, sizeof buf, 10); // 10 second timeout
33
34  if (n == -1) {
35      // error occurred
36      perror("recvtimeout");
37  }
38  else if (n == -2) {
39      // timeout occurred
40  } else {
41      // got some data in buf
42  }
43  .
44  .
45  .
```

Notice that `recvtimeout()` returns `-2` in case of a timeout. Why not return `0`? Well, if you recall, a return value of `0` on a call to `recv()` means that the remote side closed the connection. So that return value is already spoken for, and `-1` means "error", so I chose `-2` as my timeout indicator.

How do I encrypt or compress the data before sending it through the socket?

One easy way to do encryption is to use SSL (secure sockets layer), but that's beyond the scope of this guide. (Check out the OpenSSL project[45] for more info.)

But assuming you want to plug in or implement your own compressor or encryption system, it's just a matter of thinking of your data as running through a sequence of steps between both ends. Each step changes the data in some way.

---

[45]https://www.openssl.org/

1. server reads data from file (or wherever)
2. server encrypts/compresses data (you add this part)
3. server `send()`s encrypted data

Now the other way around:

1. client `recv()`s encrypted data
2. client decrypts/decompresses data (you add this part)
3. client writes data to file (or wherever)

If you're going to compress and encrypt, just remember to compress first. :-)

Just as long as the client properly undoes what the server does, the data will be fine in the end no matter how many intermediate steps you add.

So all you need to do to use my code is to find the place between where the data is read and the data is sent (using `send()`) over the network, and stick some code in there that does the encryption.

What is this "PF_INET" I keep seeing? Is it related to AF_INET?

Yes, yes it is. See the section on `socket()` for details.

How can I write a server that accepts shell commands from a client and executes them?

For simplicity, lets say the client `connect()`s, `send()`s, and `close()`s the connection (that is, there are no subsequent system calls without the client connecting again).

The process the client follows is this:

1. `connect()` to server
2. `send("/sbin/ls > /tmp/client.out")`
3. `close()` the connection

Meanwhile, the server is handling the data and executing it:

1. `accept()` the connection from the client
2. `recv(str)` the command string
3. `close()` the connection
4. `system(str)` to run the command

Beware! Having the server execute what the client says is like giving remote shell access and people can do things to your account when they connect to the server. For instance, in the above example, what if the client sends "`rm -rf ~`"? It deletes everything in your account, that's what!

So you get wise, and you prevent the client from using any except for a couple utilities that you know are safe, like the `foobar` utility:

```
if (!strncmp(str, "foobar", 6)) {
    sprintf(sysstr, "%s > /tmp/server.out", str);
    system(sysstr);
}
```

But you're still unsafe, unfortunately: what if the client enters "`foobar; rm -rf ~`"? The safest thing to do is to write a little routine that puts an escape ("`\`") character in front of all non-alphanumeric characters (including spaces, if appropriate) in the arguments for the command.

As you can see, security is a pretty big issue when the server starts executing things the client sends.

I'm sending a slew of data, but when I `recv()`, it only receives 536 bytes or 1460 bytes at a time. But if I run it on my local machine, it receives all the data at the same time. What's going on?

You're hitting the MTU—the maximum size the physical medium can handle. On the local machine, you're using the loopback device which can handle 8K or more no problem. But on Ethernet, which can only handle 1500 bytes with a header, you hit that limit. Over a modem, with 576 MTU (again, with header), you hit the even lower limit.

You have to make sure all the data is being sent, first of all. (See the `sendall()` function implementation for details.) Once you're sure of that, then you need to call `recv()` in a loop until all your data is read.

Read the section Son of Data Encapsulation for details on receiving complete packets of data using multiple calls to `recv()`.

I'm on a Windows box and I don't have the `fork()` system call or any kind of `struct sigaction`. What to do?

If they're anywhere, they'll be in POSIX libraries that may have shipped with your compiler. Since I don't have a Windows box, I really can't tell you the answer, but I seem to remember that Microsoft has a POSIX compatibility layer and that's where `fork()` would be. (And maybe even `sigaction`.)

Search the help that came with VC++ for "fork" or "POSIX" and see if it gives you any clues.

If that doesn't work at all, ditch the `fork()`/`sigaction` stuff and replace it with the Win32 equivalent: `CreateProcess()`. I don't know how to use `CreateProcess()`—it takes a bazillion arguments, but it should be covered in the docs that came with VC++.

I'm behind a firewall—how do I let people outside the firewall know my IP address so they can connect to my machine?

Unfortunately, the purpose of a firewall is to prevent people outside the firewall from connecting to machines inside the firewall, so allowing them to do so is basically considered a breach of security.

This isn't to say that all is lost. For one thing, you can still often `connect()` through the firewall if it's doing some kind of masquerading or NAT or something like that. Just design your programs so that you're always the one initiating the connection, and you'll be fine.

If that's not satisfactory, you can ask your sysadmins to poke a hole in the firewall so that people can connect to you. The firewall can forward to you either through it's NAT software, or through a proxy or something like that.

Be aware that a hole in the firewall is nothing to be taken lightly. You have to make sure you don't give bad people access to the internal network; if you're a beginner, it's a lot harder to make software secure than you might imagine.

Don't make your sysadmin mad at me. ;-)

How do I write a packet sniffer? How do I put my Ethernet interface into promiscuous mode?

For those not in the know, when a network card is in "promiscuous mode", it will forward ALL packets to the operating system, not just those that were addressed to this particular machine. (We're talking Ethernet-layer addresses here, not IP addresses–but since ethernet is lower-layer than IP, all IP addresses are effectively forwarded as well. See the section Low Level Nonsense and Network Theory for more info.)

This is the basis for how a packet sniffer works. It puts the interface into promiscuous mode, then the OS gets every single packet that goes by on the wire. You'll have a socket of some type that you can read this data from.

Unfortunately, the answer to the question varies depending on the platform, but if you Google for, for instance, "windows promiscuous ioctl" you'll probably get somewhere. For Linux, there's what looks like a useful Stack Overflow thread[46], as well.

How can I set a custom timeout value for a TCP or UDP socket?

It depends on your system. You might search the net for `SO_RCVTIMEO` and `SO_SNDTIMEO` (for use with `setsockopt()`) to see if your system supports such functionality.

The Linux man page suggests using `alarm()` or `setitimer()` as a substitute.

How can I tell which ports are available to use? Is there a list of "official" port numbers?

Usually this isn't an issue. If you're writing, say, a web server, then it's a good idea to use the well-known port 80 for your software. If you're writing just your own specialized server, then choose a port at random (but greater than 1023) and give it a try.

---

[46]https://stackoverflow.com/questions/21323023/

If the port is already in use, you'll get an "Address already in use" error when you try to `bind()`. Choose another port. (It's a good idea to allow the user of your software to specify an alternate port either with a config file or a command line switch.)

There is a list of official port numbers[47] maintained by the Internet Assigned Numbers Authority (IANA). Just because something (over 1023) is in that list doesn't mean you can't use the port. For instance, Id Software's DOOM uses the same port as "mdqs", whatever that is. All that matters is that no one else *on the same machine* is using that port when you want to use it.

---

[47] https://www.iana.org/assignments/port-numbers

Man Pages

In the Unix world, there are a lot of manuals. They have little sections that describe individual functions that you have at your disposal.

Of course, `manual` would be too much of a thing to type. I mean, no one in the Unix world, including myself, likes to type that much. Indeed I could go on and on at great length about how much I prefer to be terse but instead I shall be brief and not bore you with long-winded diatribes about how utterly amazingly brief I prefer to be in virtually all circumstances in their entirety.

[Applause]

Thank you. What I am getting at is that these pages are called "man pages" in the Unix world, and I have included my own personal truncated variant here for your reading enjoyment. The thing is, many of these functions are way more general purpose than I'm letting on, but I'm only going to present the parts that are relevant for Internet Sockets Programming.

But wait! That's not all that's wrong with my man pages:

- They are incomplete and only show the basics from the guide.
- There are many more man pages than this in the real world.
- They are different than the ones on your system.
- The header files might be different for certain functions on your system.
- The function parameters might be different for certain functions on your system.

If you want the real information, check your local Unix man pages by typing `man whatever`, where "whatever" is something that you're incredibly interested in, such as "accept". (I'm sure Microsoft Visual Studio has something similar in their help section. But "man" is better because it is one byte more concise than "help". Unix wins again!)

So, if these are so flawed, why even include them at all in the Guide? Well, there are a few reasons, but the best are that (a) these versions are geared specifically toward network programming and are easier to digest than the real ones, and (b) these versions contain examples!

Oh! And speaking of the examples, I don't tend to put in all the error checking because it really increases the length of the code. But you should absolutely do error checking pretty much any time you make any of the system calls unless you're totally 100% sure it's not going to fail, and you should probably do it even then!

accept()

Accept an incoming connection on a listening socket

Synopsis

```
#include <sys/types.h>
#include <sys/socket.h>

int accept(int s, struct sockaddr *addr, socklen_t *addrlen);
```

Description

Once you've gone through the trouble of getting a SOCK_STREAM socket and setting it up for incoming connections with listen(), then you call accept() to actually get yourself a new socket descriptor to use for subsequent communication with the newly connected client.

The old socket that you are using for listening is still there, and will be used for further accept() calls as they come in.

Parameter	Description
s	The listen()ing socket descriptor.
addr	This is filled in with the address of the site that's connecting to you.
addrlen	This is filled in with the sizeof() the structure returned in the addr parameter. You can safely ignore it if you assume you're getting a struct sockaddr_in back, which you know you are, because that's the type you passed in for addr.

accept() will normally block, and you can use select() to peek on the listening socket descriptor ahead of time to see if it's "ready to read". If so, then there's a new connection waiting to be accept()ed! Yay! Alternatively, you could set the O_NONBLOCK flag on the listening socket using fcntl(), and then it will never block, choosing instead to return -1 with errno set to EWOULDBLOCK.

The socket descriptor returned by accept() is a bona fide socket descriptor, open and connected to the remote host. You have to close() it when you're done with it.

Return Value

accept() returns the newly connected socket descriptor, or -1 on error, with errno set appropriately.

Example

```
1    struct sockaddr_storage their_addr;
2    socklen_t addr_size;
3    struct addrinfo hints, *res;
4    int sockfd, new_fd;
5
6    // first, load up address structs with getaddrinfo():
7
8    memset(&hints, 0, sizeof hints);
9    hints.ai_family = AF_UNSPEC;  // use IPv4 or IPv6, whichever
10   hints.ai_socktype = SOCK_STREAM;
11   hints.ai_flags = AI_PASSIVE;      // fill in my IP for me
12
13   getaddrinfo(NULL, MYPORT, &hints, &res);
14
15   // make a socket, bind it, and listen on it:
16
17   sockfd = socket(res->ai_family, res->ai_socktype, res->ai_protocol);
18   bind(sockfd, res->ai_addr, res->ai_addrlen);
19   listen(sockfd, BACKLOG);
20
21   // now accept an incoming connection:
22
23   addr_size = sizeof their_addr;
24   new_fd = accept(sockfd, (struct sockaddr *)&their_addr, &addr_size);
25
26   // ready to communicate on socket descriptor new_fd!
```

See Also

`socket()`, `getaddrinfo()`, `listen()`, `struct sockaddr_in`

bind()

Associate a socket with an IP address and port number

Synopsis

```
#include <sys/types.h>
#include <sys/socket.h>

int bind(int sockfd, struct sockaddr *my_addr, socklen_t addrlen);
```

Description

When a remote machine wants to connect to your server program, it needs two pieces of information: the IP address and the port number. The bind() call allows you to do just that.

First, you call getaddrinfo() to load up a struct sockaddr with the destination address and port information. Then you call socket() to get a socket descriptor, and then you pass the socket and address into bind(), and the IP address and port are magically (using actual magic) bound to the socket!

If you don't know your IP address, or you know you only have one IP address on the machine, or you don't care which of the machine's IP addresses is used, you can simply pass the AI_PASSIVE flag in the hints parameter to getaddrinfo(). What this does is fill in the IP address part of the struct sockaddr with a special value that tells bind() that it should automatically fill in this host's IP address.

What what? What special value is loaded into the struct sockaddr's IP address to cause it to auto-fill the address with the current host? I'll tell you, but keep in mind this is only if you're filling out the struct sockaddr by hand; if not, use the results from getaddrinfo(), as per above. In IPv4, the sin_addr.s_addr field of the struct sockaddr_in structure is set to INADDR_ANY. In IPv6, the sin6_addr field of the struct sockaddr_in6 structure is assigned into from the global variable in6addr_any. Or, if you're declaring a new struct in6_addr, you can initialize it to IN6ADDR_ANY_INIT.

Lastly, the addrlen parameter should be set to sizeof my_addr.

Return Value

Returns zero on success, or -1 on error (and errno will be set accordingly).

Example

```
1   // modern way of doing things with getaddrinfo()
2
3   struct addrinfo hints, *res;
4   int sockfd;
5
6   // first, load up address structs with getaddrinfo():
7
8   memset(&hints, 0, sizeof hints);
9   hints.ai_family = AF_UNSPEC;    // use IPv4 or IPv6, whichever
10  hints.ai_socktype = SOCK_STREAM;
11  hints.ai_flags = AI_PASSIVE;        // fill in my IP for me
12
13  getaddrinfo(NULL, "3490", &hints, &res);
14
15  // make a socket:
16  // (you should actually walk the "res" linked list and error-check!)
17
18  sockfd = socket(res->ai_family, res->ai_socktype, res->ai_protocol);
19
20  // bind it to the port we passed in to getaddrinfo():
21
22  bind(sockfd, res->ai_addr, res->ai_addrlen);
```

```
1   // example of packing a struct by hand, IPv4
2
3   struct sockaddr_in myaddr;
4   int s;
5
6   myaddr.sin_family = AF_INET;
7   myaddr.sin_port = htons(3490);
8
9   // you can specify an IP address:
10  inet_pton(AF_INET, "63.161.169.137", &(myaddr.sin_addr));
11
12  // or you can let it automatically select one:
13  myaddr.sin_addr.s_addr = INADDR_ANY;
14
15  s = socket(PF_INET, SOCK_STREAM, 0);
16  bind(s, (struct sockaddr*)&myaddr, sizeof myaddr);
```

See Also

getaddrinfo(), socket(), struct sockaddr_in, struct in_addr

connect()

Connect a socket to a server

Synopsis

```
#include <sys/types.h>
#include <sys/socket.h>

int connect(int sockfd, const struct sockaddr *serv_addr,
            socklen_t addrlen);
```

Description

Once you've built a socket descriptor with the `socket()` call, you can `connect()` that socket to a remote server using the well-named `connect()` system call. All you need to do is pass it the socket descriptor and the address of the server you're interested in getting to know better. (Oh, and the length of the address, which is commonly passed to functions like this.)

Usually this information comes along as the result of a call to `getaddrinfo()`, but you can fill out your own `struct sockaddr` if you want to.

If you haven't yet called `bind()` on the socket descriptor, it is automatically bound to your IP address and a random local port. This is usually just fine with you if you're not a server, since you really don't care what your local port is; you only care what the remote port is so you can put it in the `serv_addr` parameter. You *can* call `bind()` if you really want your client socket to be on a specific IP address and port, but this is pretty rare.

Once the socket is `connect()`ed, you're free to `send()` and `recv()` data on it to your heart's content.

Special note: if you `connect()` a SOCK_DGRAM UDP socket to a remote host, you can use `send()` and `recv()` as well as `sendto()` and `recvfrom()`. If you want.

Return Value

Returns zero on success, or `-1` on error (and `errno` will be set accordingly).

Example

```
// connect to www.example.com port 80 (http)

struct addrinfo hints, *res;
int sockfd;

```

```
6   // first, load up address structs with getaddrinfo():
7
8   memset(&hints, 0, sizeof hints);
9   hints.ai_family = AF_UNSPEC;   // use IPv4 or IPv6, whichever
10  hints.ai_socktype = SOCK_STREAM;
11
12  // we could put "80" instead on "http" on the next line:
13  getaddrinfo("www.example.com", "http", &hints, &res);
14
15  // make a socket:
16
17  sockfd = socket(res->ai_family, res->ai_socktype, res->ai_protocol);
18
19  // connect it to the address and port we passed in to getaddrinfo():
20
21  connect(sockfd, res->ai_addr, res->ai_addrlen);
```

See Also

```
socket(), bind()
```

close()

Close a socket descriptor

Synopsis

```
#include <unistd.h>

int close(int s);
```

Description

After you've finished using the socket for whatever demented scheme you have concocted and you don't want to send() or recv() or, indeed, do *anything else* at all with the socket, you can close() it, and it'll be freed up, never to be used again.

The remote side can tell if this happens one of two ways. One: if the remote side calls recv(), it will return 0. Two: if the remote side calls send(), it'll receive a signal SIGPIPE and send() will return -1 and errno will be set to EPIPE.

Windows users: the function you need to use is called closesocket(), not close(). If you try to use close() on a socket descriptor, it's possible Windows will get angry... And you wouldn't like it when it's angry.

Return Value

Returns zero on success, or -1 on error (and errno will be set accordingly).

Example

```
1  s = socket(PF_INET, SOCK_DGRAM, 0);
2  .
3  .
4  .
5  // a whole lotta stuff...*BRRRONNNN!*
6  .
7  .
8  .
9  close(s);  // not much to it, really.
```

See Also

socket(), shutdown()

getaddrinfo(), freeaddrinfo(), gai_strerror()

Get information about a host name and/or service and load up a `struct sockaddr` with the result.

Synopsis

```
#include <sys/types.h>
#include <sys/socket.h>
#include <netdb.h>

int getaddrinfo(const char *nodename, const char *servname,
                const struct addrinfo *hints, struct addrinfo **res);

void freeaddrinfo(struct addrinfo *ai);

const char *gai_strerror(int ecode);

struct addrinfo {
  int     ai_flags;      // AI_PASSIVE, AI_CANONNAME, ...
  int     ai_family;     // AF_xxx
  int     ai_socktype;   // SOCK_xxx
  int     ai_protocol;   // 0 (auto) or IPPROTO_TCP, IPPROTO_UDP

  socklen_t  ai_addrlen;     // length of ai_addr
  char    *ai_canonname;     // canonical name for nodename
  struct sockaddr   *ai_addr; // binary address
  struct addrinfo   *ai_next; // next structure in linked list
};
```

Description

getaddrinfo() is an excellent function that will return information on a particular host name (such as its IP address) and load up a `struct sockaddr` for you, taking care of the gritty details (like if it's IPv4 or IPv6). It replaces the old functions gethostbyname() and getservbyname().The description, below, contains a lot of information that might be a little daunting, but actual usage is pretty simple. It might be worth it to check out the examples first.

The host name that you're interested in goes in the nodename parameter. The address can be either a host name, like "www.example.com", or an IPv4 or IPv6 address (passed as a string). This parameter can also be NULL if you're using the AI_PASSIVE flag (see below).

The servname parameter is basically the port number. It can be a port number (passed as a string, like "80"), or it can be a service name, like "http" or "tftp" or "smtp" or "pop", etc.

Well-known service names can be found in the IANA Port List[48] or in your `/etc/services` file.

Lastly, for input parameters, we have `hints`. This is really where you get to define what the `getaddrinfo()` function is going to do. Zero the whole structure before use with `memset()`. Let's take a look at the fields you need to set up before use.

The `ai_flags` can be set to a variety of things, but here are a couple important ones. (Multiple flags can be specified by bitwise-ORing them together with the | operator). Check your man page for the complete list of flags.

`AI_CANONNAME` causes the `ai_canonname` of the result to the filled out with the host's canonical (real) name. `AI_PASSIVE` causes the result's IP address to be filled out with `INADDR_ANY` (IPv4) or `in6addr_any` (IPv6); this causes a subsequent call to `bind()` to auto-fill the IP address of the `struct sockaddr` with the address of the current host. That's excellent for setting up a server when you don't want to hardcode the address.

If you do use the `AI_PASSIVE`, flag, then you can pass `NULL` in the `nodename` (since `bind()` will fill it in for you later).

Continuing on with the input paramters, you'll likely want to set `ai_family` to `AF_UNSPEC` which tells `getaddrinfo()` to look for both IPv4 and IPv6 addresses. You can also restrict yourself to one or the other with `AF_INET` or `AF_INET6`.

Next, the `socktype` field should be set to `SOCK_STREAM` or `SOCK_DGRAM`, depending on which type of socket you want.

Finally, just leave `ai_protocol` at 0 to automatically choose your protocol type.

Now, after you get all that stuff in there, you can *finally* make the call to `getaddrinfo()`!

Of course, this is where the fun begins. The `res` will now point to a linked list of `struct addrinfos`, and you can go through this list to get all the addresses that match what you passed in with the hints.

Now, it's possible to get some addresses that don't work for one reason or another, so what the Linux man page does is loops through the list doing a call to `socket()` and `connect()` (or `bind()` if you're setting up a server with the `AI_PASSIVE` flag) until it succeeds.

Finally, when you're done with the linked list, you need to call `freeaddrinfo()` to free up the memory (or it will be leaked, and Some People will get upset).

Return Value

Returns zero on success, or nonzero on error. If it returns nonzero, you can use the function `gai_strerror()` to get a printable version of the error code in the return value.

---

[48] https://www.iana.org/assignments/port-numbers

Example

```
1    // code for a client connecting to a server
2    // namely a stream socket to www.example.com on port 80 (http)
3    // either IPv4 or IPv6
4
5    int sockfd;
6    struct addrinfo hints, *servinfo, *p;
7    int rv;
8
9    memset(&hints, 0, sizeof hints);
10   hints.ai_family = AF_UNSPEC; // use AF_INET6 to force IPv6
11   hints.ai_socktype = SOCK_STREAM;
12
13   if ((rv = getaddrinfo("www.example.com", "http", &hints, &servinfo)) != 0) {
14       fprintf(stderr, "getaddrinfo: %s\n", gai_strerror(rv));
15       exit(1);
16   }
17
18   // loop through all the results and connect to the first we can
19   for(p = servinfo; p != NULL; p = p->ai_next) {
20       if ((sockfd = socket(p->ai_family, p->ai_socktype,
21               p->ai_protocol)) == -1) {
22           perror("socket");
23           continue;
24       }
25
26       if (connect(sockfd, p->ai_addr, p->ai_addrlen) == -1) {
27           perror("connect");
28           close(sockfd);
29           continue;
30       }
31
32       break; // if we get here, we must have connected successfully
33   }
34
35   if (p == NULL) {
36       // looped off the end of the list with no connection
37       fprintf(stderr, "failed to connect\n");
38       exit(2);
39   }
40
41   freeaddrinfo(servinfo); // all done with this structure
```

```
1   // code for a server waiting for connections
2   // namely a stream socket on port 3490, on this host's IP
3   // either IPv4 or IPv6.
4
5   int sockfd;
6   struct addrinfo hints, *servinfo, *p;
7   int rv;
8
9   memset(&hints, 0, sizeof hints);
10  hints.ai_family = AF_UNSPEC; // use AF_INET6 to force IPv6
11  hints.ai_socktype = SOCK_STREAM;
12  hints.ai_flags = AI_PASSIVE; // use my IP address
13
14  if ((rv = getaddrinfo(NULL, "3490", &hints, &servinfo)) != 0) {
15      fprintf(stderr, "getaddrinfo: %s\n", gai_strerror(rv));
16      exit(1);
17  }
18
19  // loop through all the results and bind to the first we can
20  for(p = servinfo; p != NULL; p = p->ai_next) {
21      if ((sockfd = socket(p->ai_family, p->ai_socktype,
22              p->ai_protocol)) == -1) {
23          perror("socket");
24          continue;
25      }
26
27      if (bind(sockfd, p->ai_addr, p->ai_addrlen) == -1) {
28          close(sockfd);
29          perror("bind");
30          continue;
31      }
32
33      break; // if we get here, we must have connected successfully
34  }
35
36  if (p == NULL) {
37      // looped off the end of the list with no successful bind
38      fprintf(stderr, "failed to bind socket\n");
39      exit(2);
40  }
41
42  freeaddrinfo(servinfo); // all done with this structure
```

See Also

`gethostbyname()`, `getnameinfo()`

gethostname()

Returns the name of the system

Synopsis

```
#include <sys/unistd.h>

int gethostname(char *name, size_t len);
```

Description

Your system has a name. They all do. This is a slightly more Unixy thing than the rest of the networky stuff we've been talking about, but it still has its uses.

For instance, you can get your host name, and then call `gethostbyname()` to find out your IP address.

The parameter `name` should point to a buffer that will hold the host name, and `len` is the size of that buffer in bytes. `gethostname()` won't overwrite the end of the buffer (it might return an error, or it might just stop writing), and it will NUL-terminate the string if there's room for it in the buffer.

Return Value

Returns zero on success, or `-1` on error (and `errno` will be set accordingly).

Example

```
1   char hostname[128];
2
3   gethostname(hostname, sizeof hostname);
4   printf("My hostname: %s\n", hostname);
```

See Also

`gethostbyname()`

`gethostbyname()`, `gethostbyaddr()`

Get an IP address for a hostname, or vice-versa

Synopsis

```
#include <sys/socket.h>
#include <netdb.h>

struct hostent *gethostbyname(const char *name); // DEPRECATED!
struct hostent *gethostbyaddr(const char *addr, int len, int type);
```

Description

PLEASE NOTE: these two functions are superseded by `getaddrinfo()` *and* `getnameinfo()`*!* In particular, `gethostbyname()` doesn't work well with IPv6.

These functions map back and forth between host names and IP addresses. For instance, if you have "www.example.com", you can use `gethostbyname()` to get its IP address and store it in a `struct in_addr`.

Conversely, if you have a `struct in_addr` or a `struct in6_addr`, you can use `gethostbyaddr()` to get the hostname back. `gethostbyaddr()` *is* IPv6 compatible, but you should use the newer shinier `getnameinfo()` instead.

(If you have a string containing an IP address in dots-and-numbers format that you want to look up the hostname of, you'd be better off using `getaddrinfo()` with the `AI_CANONNAME` flag.)

`gethostbyname()` takes a string like "www.yahoo.com", and returns a `struct hostent` which contains tons of information, including the IP address. (Other information is the official host name, a list of aliases, the address type, the length of the addresses, and the list of addresses—it's a general-purpose structure that's pretty easy to use for our specific purposes once you see how.)

`gethostbyaddr()` takes a `struct in_addr` or `struct in6_addr` and brings you up a corresponding host name (if there is one), so it's sort of the reverse of `gethostbyname()`. As for parameters, even though `addr` is a `char*`, you actually want to pass in a pointer to a `struct in_addr`. `len` should be `sizeof(struct in_addr)`, and `type` should be `AF_INET`.

So what is this `struct hostent` that gets returned? It has a number of fields that contain information about the host in question.

Field	Description
char *h_name	The real canonical host name.
char **h_aliases	A list of aliases that can be accessed with arrays—the last element is NULL
int h_addrtype	The result's address type, which really should be AF_INET for our purposes.
int length	The length of the addresses in bytes, which is 4 for IP (version 4) addresses.
char **h_addr_list	A list of IP addresses for this host. Although this is a char**, it's really an array of struct in_addr*s in disguise. The last array element is NULL.
h_addr	A commonly defined alias for h_addr_list[0]. If you just want any old IP address for this host (yeah, they can have more than one) just use this field.

Return Value

Returns a pointer to a resultant struct hostent on success, or NULL on error.

Instead of the normal perror() and all that stuff you'd normally use for error reporting, these functions have parallel results in the variable h_errno, which can be printed using the functions herror() or hstrerror(). These work just like the classic errno, perror(), and strerror() functions you're used to.

Example

```
1   // THIS IS A DEPRECATED METHOD OF GETTING HOST NAMES
2   // use getaddrinfo() instead!
3
4   #include <stdio.h>
5   #include <errno.h>
6   #include <netdb.h>
7   #include <sys/types.h>
8   #include <sys/socket.h>
9   #include <netinet/in.h>
10  #include <arpa/inet.h>
11
12  int main(int argc, char *argv[])
13  {
14      int i;
15      struct hostent *he;
16      struct in_addr **addr_list;
17
```

```
18    if (argc != 2) {
19        fprintf(stderr,"usage: ghbn hostname\n");
20        return 1;
21    }
22
23    if ((he = gethostbyname(argv[1])) == NULL) {  // get the host info
24        herror("gethostbyname");
25        return 2;
26    }
27
28    // print information about this host:
29    printf("Official name is: %s\n", he->h_name);
30    printf("    IP addresses: ");
31    addr_list = (struct in_addr **)he->h_addr_list;
32    for(i = 0; addr_list[i] != NULL; i++) {
33        printf("%s ", inet_ntoa(*addr_list[i]));
34    }
35    printf("\n");
36
37    return 0;
38 }
```

```
1  // THIS HAS BEEN SUPERCEDED
2  // use getnameinfo() instead!
3
4  struct hostent *he;
5  struct in_addr ipv4addr;
6  struct in6_addr ipv6addr;
7
8  inet_pton(AF_INET, "192.0.2.34", &ipv4addr);
9  he = gethostbyaddr(&ipv4addr, sizeof ipv4addr, AF_INET);
10 printf("Host name: %s\n", he->h_name);
11
12 inet_pton(AF_INET6, "2001:db8:63b3:1::beef", &ipv6addr);
13 he = gethostbyaddr(&ipv6addr, sizeof ipv6addr, AF_INET6);
14 printf("Host name: %s\n", he->h_name);
```

See Also

getaddrinfo(), getnameinfo(), gethostname(), errno, perror(), strerror(), struct in_addr

getnameinfo()

Look up the host name and service name information for a given struct sockaddr.

Synopsis

```
#include <sys/socket.h>
#include <netdb.h>

int getnameinfo(const struct sockaddr *sa, socklen_t salen,
                char *host, size_t hostlen,
                char *serv, size_t servlen, int flags);
```

Description

This function is the opposite of getaddrinfo(), that is, this function takes an already loaded struct sockaddr and does a name and service name lookup on it. It replaces the old gethostbyaddr() and getservbyport() functions.

You have to pass in a pointer to a struct sockaddr (which in actuality is probably a struct sockaddr_in or struct sockaddr_in6 that you've cast) in the sa parameter, and the length of that struct in the salen.

The resultant host name and service name will be written to the area pointed to by the host and serv parameters. Of course, you have to specify the max lengths of these buffers in hostlen and servlen.

Finally, there are several flags you can pass, but here a a couple good ones. NI_NOFQDN will cause the host to only contain the host name, not the whole domain name. NI_NAMEREQD will cause the function to fail if the name cannot be found with a DNS lookup (if you don't specify this flag and the name can't be found, getnameinfo() will put a string version of the IP address in host instead).

As always, check your local man pages for the full scoop.

Return Value

Returns zero on success, or non-zero on error. If the return value is non-zero, it can be passed to gai_strerror() to get a human-readable string. See getaddrinfo for more information.

Example

```
1  struct sockaddr_in6 sa; // could be IPv4 if you want
2  char host[1024];
3  char service[20];
```

```
4
5   // pretend sa is full of good information about the host and port...
6
7   getnameinfo(&sa, sizeof sa, host, sizeof host, service, sizeof service, 0);
8
9   printf("  host: %s\n", host);      // e.g. "www.example.com"
10  printf("service: %s\n", service); // e.g. "http"
```

See Also

getaddrinfo(), gethostbyaddr()

`getpeername()`

Return address info about the remote side of the connection

Synopsis

```
#include <sys/socket.h>

int getpeername(int s, struct sockaddr *addr, socklen_t *len);
```

Description

Once you have either `accept()`ed a remote connection, or `connect()`ed to a server, you now have what is known as a *peer*. Your peer is simply the computer you're connected to, identified by an IP address and a port. So…

`getpeername()` simply returns a `struct sockaddr_in` filled with information about the machine you're connected to.

Why is it called a "name"? Well, there are a lot of different kinds of sockets, not just Internet Sockets like we're using in this guide, and so "name" was a nice generic term that covered all cases. In our case, though, the peer's "name" is it's IP address and port.

Although the function returns the size of the resultant address in `len`, you must preload `len` with the size of `addr`.

Return Value

Returns zero on success, or `-1` on error (and `errno` will be set accordingly).

Example

```
 1  // assume s is a connected socket
 2
 3  socklen_t len;
 4  struct sockaddr_storage addr;
 5  char ipstr[INET6_ADDRSTRLEN];
 6  int port;
 7
 8  len = sizeof addr;
 9  getpeername(s, (struct sockaddr*)&addr, &len);
10
11  // deal with both IPv4 and IPv6:
12  if (addr.ss_family == AF_INET) {
13      struct sockaddr_in *s = (struct sockaddr_in *)&addr;
14      port = ntohs(s->sin_port);
```

```
15      inet_ntop(AF_INET, &s->sin_addr, ipstr, sizeof ipstr);
16  } else { // AF_INET6
17      struct sockaddr_in6 *s = (struct sockaddr_in6 *)&addr;
18      port = ntohs(s->sin6_port);
19      inet_ntop(AF_INET6, &s->sin6_addr, ipstr, sizeof ipstr);
20  }
21
22  printf("Peer IP address: %s\n", ipstr);
23  printf("Peer port      : %d\n", port);
```

See Also

gethostname(), gethostbyname(), gethostbyaddr()

errno

Holds the error code for the last system call

Synopsis

```
#include <errno.h>

int errno;
```

Description

This is the variable that holds error information for a lot of system calls. If you'll recall, things like `socket()` and `listen()` return `-1` on error, and they set the exact value of `errno` to let you know specifically which error occurred.

The header file `errno.h` lists a bunch of constant symbolic names for errors, such as EAD-DRINUSE, EPIPE, ECONNREFUSED, etc. Your local man pages will tell you what codes can be returned as an error, and you can use these at run time to handle different errors in different ways.

Or, more commonly, you can call `perror()` or `strerror()` to get a human-readable version of the error.

One thing to note, for you multithreading enthusiasts, is that on most systems `errno` is defined in a threadsafe manner. (That is, it's not actually a global variable, but it behaves just like a global variable would in a single-threaded environment.)

Return Value

The value of the variable is the latest error to have transpired, which might be the code for "success" if the last action succeeded.

Example

```
1   s = socket(PF_INET, SOCK_STREAM, 0);
2   if (s == -1) {
3       perror("socket"); // or use strerror()
4   }
5
6   tryagain:
7   if (select(n, &readfds, NULL, NULL) == -1) {
8       // an error has occurred!!
9
10      // if we were only interrupted, just restart the select() call:
11      if (errno == EINTR) goto tryagain;  // AAAA! goto!!!
```

```
12
13        // otherwise it's a more serious error:
14        perror("select");
15        exit(1);
16    }
```

See Also

```
perror(), strerror()
```

fcntl()

Control socket descriptors

Synopsis

```
#include <sys/unistd.h>
#include <sys/fcntl.h>

int fcntl(int s, int cmd, long arg);
```

Description

This function is typically used to do file locking and other file-oriented stuff, but it also has a couple socket-related functions that you might see or use from time to time.

Parameter s is the socket descriptor you wish to operate on, cmd should be set to F_SETFL, and arg can be one of the following commands. (Like I said, there's more to fcntl() than I'm letting on here, but I'm trying to stay socket-oriented.)

cmd	Description
O_NONBLOCK	Set the socket to be non-blocking. See the section on blocking for more details.
O_ASYNC	Set the socket to do asynchronous I/O. When data is ready to be recv()'d on the socket, the signal SIGIO will be raised. This is rare to see, and beyond the scope of the guide. And I think it's only available on certain systems.

Return Value

Returns zero on success, or -1 on error (and errno will be set accordingly).

Different uses of the fcntl() system call actually have different return values, but I haven't covered them here because they're not socket-related. See your local fcntl() man page for more information.

Example

```
1  int s = socket(PF_INET, SOCK_STREAM, 0);
2
3  fcntl(s, F_SETFL, O_NONBLOCK);  // set to non-blocking
4  fcntl(s, F_SETFL, O_ASYNC);     // set to asynchronous I/O
```

See Also

Blocking, send( )

`htons()`, `htonl()`, `ntohs()`, `ntohl()`

Convert multi-byte integer types from host byte order to network byte order

Synopsis

```
#include <netinet/in.h>

uint32_t htonl(uint32_t hostlong);
uint16_t htons(uint16_t hostshort);
uint32_t ntohl(uint32_t netlong);
uint16_t ntohs(uint16_t netshort);
```

Description

Just to make you really unhappy, different computers use different byte orderings internally for their multibyte integers (i.e. any integer that's larger than a `char`). The upshot of this is that if you `send()` a two-byte `short int` from an Intel box to a Mac (before they became Intel boxes, too, I mean), what one computer thinks is the number 1, the other will think is the number 256, and vice-versa.

The way to get around this problem is for everyone to put aside their differences and agree that Motorola and IBM had it right, and Intel did it the weird way, and so we all convert our byte orderings to "big-endian" before sending them out. Since Intel is a "little-endian" machine, it's far more politically correct to call our preferred byte ordering "Network Byte Order". So these functions convert from your native byte order to network byte order and back again.

(This means on Intel these functions swap all the bytes around, and on PowerPC they do nothing because the bytes are already in Network Byte Order. But you should always use them in your code anyway, since someone might want to build it on an Intel machine and still have things work properly.)

Note that the types involved are 32-bit (4 byte, probably `int`) and 16-bit (2 byte, very likely `short`) numbers. 64-bit machines might have a `htonll()` for 64-bit `int`s, but I've not seen it. You'll just have to write your own.

Anyway, the way these functions work is that you first decide if you're converting *from* host (your machine's) byte order or from network byte order. If "host", the the first letter of the function you're going to call is "h". Otherwise it's "n" for "network". The middle of the function name is always "to" because you're converting from one "to" another, and the penultimate letter shows what you're converting *to*. The last letter is the size of the data, "s" for short, or "l" for long. Thus:

Function	Description
htons()	host to network short
htonl()	host to network long
ntohs()	network to host short
ntohl()	network to host long

Return Value

Each function returns the converted value.

Example

```
1   uint32_t some_long = 10;
2   uint16_t some_short = 20;
3
4   uint32_t network_byte_order;
5
6   // convert and send
7   network_byte_order = htonl(some_long);
8   send(s, &network_byte_order, sizeof(uint32_t), 0);
9
10  some_short == ntohs(htons(some_short)); // this expression is true
```

inet_ntoa(), inet_aton(), inet_addr

Convert IP addresses from a dots-and-number string to a struct in_addr and back

Synopsis

```
#include <sys/socket.h>
#include <netinet/in.h>
#include <arpa/inet.h>

// ALL THESE ARE DEPRECATED! Use inet_pton() or inet_ntop() instead!!

char *inet_ntoa(struct in_addr in);
int inet_aton(const char *cp, struct in_addr *inp);
in_addr_t inet_addr(const char *cp);
```

Description

These functions are deprecated because they don't handle IPv6! Use inet_ntop() or inet_pton() instead! They are included here because they can still be found in the wild.

All of these functions convert from a struct in_addr (part of your struct sockaddr_in, most likely) to a string in dots-and-numbers format (e.g. "192.168.5.10") and vice-versa. If you have an IP address passed on the command line or something, this is the easiest way to get a struct in_addr to connect() to, or whatever. If you need more power, try some of the DNS functions like gethostbyname() or attempt a *coup d'État* in your local country.

The function inet_ntoa() converts a network address in a struct in_addr to a dots-and-numbers format string. The "n" in "ntoa" stands for network, and the "a" stands for ASCII for historical reasons (so it's "Network To ASCII"—the "toa" suffix has an analogous friend in the C library called atoi() which converts an ASCII string to an integer).

The function inet_aton() is the opposite, converting from a dots-and-numbers string into a in_addr_t (which is the type of the field s_addr in your struct in_addr).

Finally, the function inet_addr() is an older function that does basically the same thing as inet_aton(). It's theoretically deprecated, but you'll see it a lot and the police won't come get you if you use it.

Return Value

inet_aton() returns non-zero if the address is a valid one, and it returns zero if the address is invalid.

inet_ntoa() returns the dots-and-numbers string in a static buffer that is overwritten with each call to the function.

`inet_addr()` returns the address as an `in_addr_t`, or `-1` if there's an error. (That is the same result as if you tried to convert the string "`255.255.255.255`", which is a valid IP address. This is why `inet_aton()` is better.)

Example

```
struct sockaddr_in antelope;
char *some_addr;

inet_aton("10.0.0.1", &antelope.sin_addr); // store IP in antelope

some_addr = inet_ntoa(antelope.sin_addr); // return the IP
printf("%s\n", some_addr); // prints "10.0.0.1"

// and this call is the same as the inet_aton() call, above:
antelope.sin_addr.s_addr = inet_addr("10.0.0.1");
```

See Also

`inet_ntop()`, `inet_pton()`, `gethostbyname()`, `gethostbyaddr()`

`inet_ntop()`, `inet_pton()`

Convert IP addresses to human-readable form and back.

Synopsis

```
#include <arpa/inet.h>

const char *inet_ntop(int af, const void *src,
                      char *dst, socklen_t size);

int inet_pton(int af, const char *src, void *dst);
```

Description

These functions are for dealing with human-readable IP addresses and converting them to their binary representation for use with various functions and system calls. The "n" stands for "network", and "p" for "presentation". Or "text presentation". But you can think of it as "printable". "ntop" is "network to printable". See?

Sometimes you don't want to look at a pile of binary numbers when looking at an IP address. You want it in a nice printable form, like `192.0.2.180`, or `2001:db8:8714:3a90::12`. In that case, `inet_ntop()` is for you.

`inet_ntop()` takes the address family in the `af` parameter (either `AF_INET` or `AF_INET6`). The `src` parameter should be a pointer to either a `struct in_addr` or `struct in6_addr` containing the address you wish to convert to a string. Finally `dst` and `size` are the pointer to the destination string and the maximum length of that string.

What should the maximum length of the `dst` string be? What is the maximum length for IPv4 and IPv6 addresses? Fortunately there are a couple of macros to help you out. The maximum lengths are: `INET_ADDRSTRLEN` and `INET6_ADDRSTRLEN`.

Other times, you might have a string containing an IP address in readable form, and you want to pack it into a `struct sockaddr_in` or a `struct sockaddr_in6`. In that case, the opposite funcion `inet_pton()` is what you're after.

`inet_pton()` also takes an address family (either `AF_INET` or `AF_INET6`) in the `af` parameter. The `src` parameter is a pointer to a string containing the IP address in printable form. Lastly the `dst` parameter points to where the result should be stored, which is probably a `struct in_addr` or `struct in6_addr`.

These functions don't do DNS lookups—you'll need `getaddrinfo()` for that.

Return Value

`inet_ntop()` returns the `dst` parameter on success, or `NULL` on failure (and `errno` is set).

inet_pton() returns 1 on success. It returns -1 if there was an error (errno is set), or 0 if the input isn't a valid IP address.

Example

```
// IPv4 demo of inet_ntop() and inet_pton()

struct sockaddr_in sa;
char str[INET_ADDRSTRLEN];

// store this IP address in sa:
inet_pton(AF_INET, "192.0.2.33", &(sa.sin_addr));

// now get it back and print it
inet_ntop(AF_INET, &(sa.sin_addr), str, INET_ADDRSTRLEN);

printf("%s\n", str); // prints "192.0.2.33"
```

```
// IPv6 demo of inet_ntop() and inet_pton()
// (basically the same except with a bunch of 6s thrown around)

struct sockaddr_in6 sa;
char str[INET6_ADDRSTRLEN];

// store this IP address in sa:
inet_pton(AF_INET6, "2001:db8:8714:3a90::12", &(sa.sin6_addr));

// now get it back and print it
inet_ntop(AF_INET6, &(sa.sin6_addr), str, INET6_ADDRSTRLEN);

printf("%s\n", str); // prints "2001:db8:8714:3a90::12"
```

```
// Helper function you can use:

//Convert a struct sockaddr address to a string, IPv4 and IPv6:

char *get_ip_str(const struct sockaddr *sa, char *s, size_t maxlen)
{
    switch(sa->sa_family) {
        case AF_INET:
            inet_ntop(AF_INET, &(((struct sockaddr_in *)sa)->sin_addr),
                    s, maxlen);
            break;

        case AF_INET6:
```

```
14              inet_ntop(AF_INET6, &(((struct sockaddr_in6 *)sa)->sin6_addr),
15                      s, maxlen);
16              break;
17
18          default:
19              strncpy(s, "Unknown AF", maxlen);
20              return NULL;
21      }
22
23      return s;
24  }
```

See Also

getaddrinfo()

`listen()`

Tell a socket to listen for incoming connections

Synopsis

```
#include <sys/socket.h>

int listen(int s, int backlog);
```

Description

You can take your socket descriptor (made with the `socket()` system call) and tell it to listen for incoming connections. This is what differentiates the servers from the clients, guys.

The `backlog` parameter can mean a couple different things depending on the system you on, but loosely it is how many pending connections you can have before the kernel starts rejecting new ones. So as the new connections come in, you should be quick to `accept()` them so that the backlog doesn't fill. Try setting it to 10 or so, and if your clients start getting "Connection refused" under heavy load, set it higher.

Before calling `listen()`, your server should call `bind()` to attach itself to a specific port number. That port number (on the server's IP address) will be the one that clients connect to.

Return Value

Returns zero on success, or `-1` on error (and `errno` will be set accordingly).

Example

```
1   struct addrinfo hints, *res;
2   int sockfd;
3
4   // first, load up address structs with getaddrinfo():
5
6   memset(&hints, 0, sizeof hints);
7   hints.ai_family = AF_UNSPEC;   // use IPv4 or IPv6, whichever
8   hints.ai_socktype = SOCK_STREAM;
9   hints.ai_flags = AI_PASSIVE;      // fill in my IP for me
10
11  getaddrinfo(NULL, "3490", &hints, &res);
12
13  // make a socket:
```

```
14
15   sockfd = socket(res->ai_family, res->ai_socktype, res->ai_protocol);
16
17   // bind it to the port we passed in to getaddrinfo():
18
19   bind(sockfd, res->ai_addr, res->ai_addrlen);
20
21   listen(sockfd, 10); // set s up to be a server (listening) socket
22
23   // then have an accept() loop down here somewhere
```

See Also

`accept()`, `bind()`, `socket()`

`perror()`, `strerror()`

Print an error as a human-readable string

Synopsis

```
#include <stdio.h>
#include <string.h>   // for strerror()

void perror(const char *s);
char *strerror(int errnum);
```

Description

Since so many functions return -1 on error and set the value of the variable errno to be some number, it would sure be nice if you could easily print that in a form that made sense to you.

Mercifully, perror() does that. If you want more description to be printed before the error, you can point the parameter s to it (or you can leave s as NULL and nothing additional will be printed).

In a nutshell, this function takes errno values, like ECONNRESET, and prints them nicely, like "Connection reset by peer."

The function strerror() is very similar to perror(), except it returns a pointer to the error message string for a given value (you usually pass in the variable errno).

Return Value

strerror() returns a pointer to the error message string.

Example

```
 1  int s;
 2
 3  s = socket(PF_INET, SOCK_STREAM, 0);
 4
 5  if (s == -1) { // some error has occurred
 6      // prints "socket error: " + the error message:
 7      perror("socket error");
 8  }
 9
10  // similarly:
11  if (listen(s, 10) == -1) {
12      // this prints "an error: " + the error message from errno:
```

```
13      printf("an error: %s\n", strerror(errno));
14  }
```

See Also

errno

poll()

Test for events on multiple sockets simultaneously

Synopsis

```
#include <sys/poll.h>

int poll(struct pollfd *ufds, unsigned int nfds, int timeout);
```

Description

This function is very similar to select() in that they both watch sets of file descriptors for events, such as incoming data ready to recv(), socket ready to send() data to, out-of-band data ready to recv(), errors, etc.

The basic idea is that you pass an array of nfds struct pollfds in ufds, along with a timeout in milliseconds (1000 milliseconds in a second). The timeout can be negative if you want to wait forever. If no event happens on any of the socket descriptors by the timeout, poll() will return.

Each element in the array of struct pollfds represents one socket descriptor, and contains the following fields:

```
struct pollfd {
    int fd;          // the socket descriptor
    short events;    // bitmap of events we're interested in
    short revents;   // when poll() returns, bitmap of events that occurred
};
```

Before calling poll(), load fd with the socket descriptor (if you set fd to a negative number, this struct pollfd is ignored and its revents field is set to zero) and then construct the events field by bitwise-ORing the following macros:

Macro	Description
POLLIN	Alert me when data is ready to recv() on this socket.
POLLOUT	Alert me when I can send() data to this socket without blocking.
POLLPRI	Alert me when out-of-band data is ready to recv() on this socket.

Once the poll() call returns, the revents field will be constructed as a bitwise-OR of the above fields, telling you which descriptors actually have had that event occur. Additionally, these other fields might be present:

Macro	Description
POLLERR	An error has occurred on this socket.
POLLHUP	The remote side of the connection hung up.
POLLNVAL	Something was wrong with the socket descriptor fd—maybe it's uninitialized?

Return Value

Returns the number of elements in the ufds array that have had event occur on them; this can be zero if the timeout occurred. Also returns -1 on error (and errno will be set accordingly).

Example

```
int s1, s2;
int rv;
char buf1[256], buf2[256];
struct pollfd ufds[2];

s1 = socket(PF_INET, SOCK_STREAM, 0);
s2 = socket(PF_INET, SOCK_STREAM, 0);

// pretend we've connected both to a server at this point
//connect(s1, ...)...
//connect(s2, ...)...

// set up the array of file descriptors.
//       .
// in this example, we want to know when there's normal or out-of-band
// data ready to be recv()'d...

ufds[0].fd = s1;
ufds[0].events = POLLIN | POLLPRI; // check for normal or out-of-band

ufds[1].fd = s2;
ufds[1].events = POLLIN; // check for just normal data

// wait for events on the sockets, 3.5 second timeout
rv = poll(ufds, 2, 3500);

if (rv == -1) {
    perror("poll"); // error occurred in poll()
} else if (rv == 0) {
    printf("Timeout occurred! No data after 3.5 seconds.\n");
```

```
31  } else {
32      // check for events on s1:
33      if (ufds[0].revents & POLLIN) {
34          recv(s1, buf1, sizeof buf1, 0); // receive normal data
35      }
36      if (ufds[0].revents & POLLPRI) {
37          recv(s1, buf1, sizeof buf1, MSG_OOB); // out-of-band data
38      }
39
40      // check for events on s2:
41      if (ufds[1].revents & POLLIN) {
42          recv(s1, buf2, sizeof buf2, 0);
43      }
44  }
```

See Also

```
select()
```

recv( ), recvfrom( )

Receive data on a socket

Synopsis

```
#include <sys/types.h>
#include <sys/socket.h>

ssize_t recv(int s, void *buf, size_t len, int flags);
ssize_t recvfrom(int s, void *buf, size_t len, int flags,
                 struct sockaddr *from, socklen_t *fromlen);
```

Description

Once you have a socket up and connected, you can read incoming data from the remote side using the recv( ) (for TCP SOCK_STREAM sockets) and recvfrom( ) (for UDP SOCK_DGRAM sockets).

Both functions take the socket descriptor s, a pointer to the buffer buf, the size (in bytes) of the buffer len, and a set of flags that control how the functions work.

Additionally, the recvfrom( ) takes a struct sockaddr*, from that will tell you where the data came from, and will fill in fromlen with the size of struct sockaddr. (You must also initialize fromlen to be the size of from or struct sockaddr.)

So what wondrous flags can you pass into this function? Here are some of them, but you should check your local man pages for more information and what is actually supported on your system. You bitwise-or these together, or just set flags to 0 if you want it to be a regular vanilla recv( ).

Macro	Description
MSG_OOB	Receive Out of Band data. This is how to get data that has been sent to you with the MSG_OOB flag in send( ). As the receiving side, you will have had signal SIGURG raised telling you there is urgent data. In your handler for that signal, you could call recv( ) with this MSG_OOB flag.
MSG_PEEK	If you want to call recv( ) "just for pretend", you can call it with this flag. This will tell you what's waiting in the buffer for when you call recv( ) "for real" (i.e. *without* the MSG_PEEK flag. It's like a sneak preview into the next recv( ) call.
MSG_WAITALL	Tell recv( ) to not return until all the data you specified in the len parameter. It will ignore your wishes in extreme circumstances, however, like if a signal interrupts the call or if some error occurs or if the remote side closes the connection, etc. Don't be mad with it.

When you call `recv()`, it will block until there is some data to read. If you want to not block, set the socket to non-blocking or check with `select()` or `poll()` to see if there is incoming data before calling `recv()` or `recvfrom()`.

Return Value

Returns the number of bytes actually received (which might be less than you requested in the `len` parameter), or `-1` on error (and `errno` will be set accordingly).

If the remote side has closed the connection, `recv()` will return `0`. This is the normal method for determining if the remote side has closed the connection. Normality is good, rebel!

Example

```
1   // stream sockets and recv()
2
3   struct addrinfo hints, *res;
4   int sockfd;
5   char buf[512];
6   int byte_count;
7
8   // get host info, make socket, and connect it
9   memset(&hints, 0, sizeof hints);
10  hints.ai_family = AF_UNSPEC;   // use IPv4 or IPv6, whichever
11  hints.ai_socktype = SOCK_STREAM;
12  getaddrinfo("www.example.com", "3490", &hints, &res);
13  sockfd = socket(res->ai_family, res->ai_socktype, res->ai_protocol);
14  connect(sockfd, res->ai_addr, res->ai_addrlen);
15
16  // all right! now that we're connected, we can receive some data!
17  byte_count = recv(sockfd, buf, sizeof buf, 0);
18  printf("recv()'d %d bytes of data in buf\n", byte_count);
```

```
1   // datagram sockets and recvfrom()
2
3   struct addrinfo hints, *res;
4   int sockfd;
5   int byte_count;
6   socklen_t fromlen;
7   struct sockaddr_storage addr;
8   char buf[512];
9   char ipstr[INET6_ADDRSTRLEN];
10
11  // get host info, make socket, bind it to port 4950
```

```
12   memset(&hints, 0, sizeof hints);
13   hints.ai_family = AF_UNSPEC;  // use IPv4 or IPv6, whichever
14   hints.ai_socktype = SOCK_DGRAM;
15   hints.ai_flags = AI_PASSIVE;
16   getaddrinfo(NULL, "4950", &hints, &res);
17   sockfd = socket(res->ai_family, res->ai_socktype, res->ai_protocol);
18   bind(sockfd, res->ai_addr, res->ai_addrlen);
19
20   // no need to accept(), just recvfrom():
21
22   fromlen = sizeof addr;
23   byte_count = recvfrom(sockfd, buf, sizeof buf, 0, &addr, &fromlen);
24
25   printf("recv()'d %d bytes of data in buf\n", byte_count);
26   printf("from IP address %s\n",
27       inet_ntop(addr.ss_family,
28           addr.ss_family == AF_INET?
29               ((struct sockadd_in *)&addr)->sin_addr:
30               ((struct sockadd_in6 *)&addr)->sin6_addr,
31           ipstr, sizeof ipstr);
```

See Also

send( ), sendto( ), select( ), poll( ), Blocking

`select()`

Check if sockets descriptors are ready to read/write

Synopsis

```
#include <sys/select.h>

int select(int n, fd_set *readfds, fd_set *writefds, fd_set *exceptfds,
           struct timeval *timeout);

FD_SET(int fd, fd_set *set);
FD_CLR(int fd, fd_set *set);
FD_ISSET(int fd, fd_set *set);
FD_ZERO(fd_set *set);
```

Description

The `select()` function gives you a way to simultaneously check multiple sockets to see if they have data waiting to be `recv()`d, or if you can `send()` data to them without blocking, or if some exception has occurred.

You populate your sets of socket descriptors using the macros, like `FD_SET()`, above. Once you have the set, you pass it into the function as one of the following parameters: `readfds` if you want to know when any of the sockets in the set is ready to `recv()` data, `writefds` if any of the sockets is ready to `send()` data to, and/or `exceptfds` if you need to know when an exception (error) occurs on any of the sockets. Any or all of these parameters can be `NULL` if you're not interested in those types of events. After `select()` returns, the values in the sets will be changed to show which are ready for reading or writing, and which have exceptions.

The first parameter, n is the highest-numbered socket descriptor (they're just `ints`, remember?) plus one.

Lastly, the `struct timeval`, `timeout`, at the end—this lets you tell `select()` how long to check these sets for. It'll return after the timeout, or when an event occurs, whichever is first. The `struct timeval` has two fields: `tv_sec` is the number of seconds, to which is added `tv_usec`, the number of microseconds (1,000,000 microseconds in a second).

The helper macros do the following:

Macro	Description
FD_SET(int fd, fd_set *set);	Add fd to the set.
FD_CLR(int fd, fd_set *set);	Remove fd from the set.
FD_ISSET(int fd, fd_set *set);	Return true if fd is in the set.
FD_ZERO(fd_set *set);	Clear all entries from the set.

Note for Linux users: Linux's select() can return "ready-to-read" and then not actually be ready to read, thus causing the subsequent read() call to block. You can work around this bug by setting O_NONBLOCK flag on the receiving socket so it errors with EWOULDBLOCK, then ignoring this error if it occurs. See the fcntl() reference page for more info on setting a socket to non-blocking.

Return Value

Returns the number of descriptors in the set on success, 0 if the timeout was reached, or -1 on error (and errno will be set accordingly). Also, the sets are modified to show which sockets are ready.

Example

```
int s1, s2, n;
fd_set readfds;
struct timeval tv;
char buf1[256], buf2[256];

// pretend we've connected both to a server at this point
//s1 = socket(...);
//s2 = socket(...);
//connect(s1, ...)...
//connect(s2, ...)...

// clear the set ahead of time
FD_ZERO(&readfds);

// add our descriptors to the set
FD_SET(s1, &readfds);
FD_SET(s2, &readfds);

// since we got s2 second, it's the "greater", so we use that for
// the n param in select()
n = s2 + 1;

```

```
23   // wait until either socket has data ready to be recv()d (timeout 10.5 secs)
24   tv.tv_sec = 10;
25   tv.tv_usec = 500000;
26   rv = select(n, &readfds, NULL, NULL, &tv);
27
28   if (rv == -1) {
29       perror("select"); // error occurred in select()
30   } else if (rv == 0) {
31       printf("Timeout occurred! No data after 10.5 seconds.\n");
32   } else {
33       // one or both of the descriptors have data
34       if (FD_ISSET(s1, &readfds)) {
35           recv(s1, buf1, sizeof buf1, 0);
36       }
37       if (FD_ISSET(s2, &readfds)) {
38           recv(s2, buf2, sizeof buf2, 0);
39       }
40   }
```

See Also

poll()

`setsockopt()`, `getsockopt()`

Set various options for a socket

Synopsis

```
#include <sys/types.h>
#include <sys/socket.h>

int getsockopt(int s, int level, int optname, void *optval,
               socklen_t *optlen);
int setsockopt(int s, int level, int optname, const void *optval,
               socklen_t optlen);
```

Description

Sockets are fairly configurable beasts. In fact, they are so configurable, I'm not even going to cover it all here. It's probably system-dependent anyway. But I will talk about the basics.

Obviously, these functions get and set certain options on a socket. On a Linux box, all the socket information is in the man page for socket in section 7. (Type: "man 7 socket" to get all these goodies.)

As for parameters, s is the socket you're talking about, level should be set to SOL_SOCKET. Then you set the optname to the name you're interested in. Again, see your man page for all the options, but here are some of the most fun ones:

optname	Description
SO_BINDTODEVICE	Bind this socket to a symbolic device name like eth0 instead of using bind() to bind it to an IP address. Type the command ifconfig under Unix to see the device names.
SO_REUSEADDR	Allows other sockets to bind() to this port, unless there is an active listening socket bound to the port already. This enables you to get around those "Address already in use" error messages when you try to restart your server after a crash.
SOCK_DGRAM	Allows UDP datagram (SOCK_DGRAM) sockets to send and receive packets sent to and from the broadcast address. Does nothing—*NOTHING!!*—to TCP stream sockets! Hahaha!

As for the parameter optval, it's usually a pointer to an int indicating the value in question. For booleans, zero is false, and non-zero is true. And that's an absolute fact, unless it's different on your system. If there is no parameter to be passed, optval can be NULL.

The final parameter, optlen, should be set to the length of optval, probably sizeof(int), but varies depending on the option. Note that in the case of `getsockopt()`, this is a pointer to a `socklen_t`, and it specifies the maximum size object that will be stored in `optval` (to prevent buffer overflows). And `getsockopt()` will modify the value of `optlen` to reflect the number of bytes actually set.

Warning: on some systems (notably Sun and Windows), the option can be a `char` instead of an `int`, and is set to, for example, a character value of `'1'` instead of an `int` value of 1. Again, check your own man pages for more info with "man `setsockopt`" and "man 7 `socket`"!

Return Value

Returns zero on success, or `-1` on error (and `errno` will be set accordingly).

Example

```
1   int optval;
2   int optlen;
3   char *optval2;
4
5   // set SO_REUSEADDR on a socket to true (1):
6   optval = 1;
7   setsockopt(s1, SOL_SOCKET, SO_REUSEADDR, &optval, sizeof optval);
8
9   // bind a socket to a device name (might not work on all systems):
10  optval2 = "eth1"; // 4 bytes long, so 4, below:
11  setsockopt(s2, SOL_SOCKET, SO_BINDTODEVICE, optval2, 4);
12
13  // see if the SO_BROADCAST flag is set:
14  getsockopt(s3, SOL_SOCKET, SO_BROADCAST, &optval, &optlen);
15  if (optval != 0) {
16      print("SO_BROADCAST enabled on s3!\n");
17  }
```

See Also

`fcntl()`

send(), sendto()

Send data out over a socket

Synopsis

```
#include <sys/types.h>
#include <sys/socket.h>

ssize_t send(int s, const void *buf, size_t len, int flags);
ssize_t sendto(int s, const void *buf, size_t len,
               int flags, const struct sockaddr *to,
               socklen_t tolen);
```

Description

These functions send data to a socket. Generally speaking, send() is used for TCP SOCK_STREAM connected sockets, and sendto() is used for UDP SOCK_DGRAM unconnected datagram sockets. With the unconnected sockets, you must specify the destination of a packet each time you send one, and that's why the last parameters of sendto() define where the packet is going.

With both send() and sendto(), the parameter s is the socket, buf is a pointer to the data you want to send, len is the number of bytes you want to send, and flags allows you to specify more information about how the data is to be sent. Set flags to zero if you want it to be "normal" data. Here are some of the commonly used flags, but check your local send() man pages for more details:

Macro	Description
MSG_OOB	Send as "out of band" data. TCP supports this, and it's a way to tell the receiving system that this data has a higher priority than the normal data. The receiver will receive the signal SIGURG and it can then receive this data without first receiving all the rest of the normal data in the queue.
MSG_DONTROUTE	Don't send this data over a router, just keep it local.
MSG_DONTWAIT	If send() would block because outbound traffic is clogged, have it return EAGAIN. This is like a "enable non-blocking just for this send." See the section on blocking for more details.
MSG_NOSIGNAL	If you send() to a remote host which is no longer recv()ing, you'll typically get the signal SIGPIPE. Adding this flag prevents that signal from being raised.

Return Value

Returns the number of bytes actually sent, or -1 on error (and `errno` will be set accordingly). Note that the number of bytes actually sent might be less than the number you asked it to send! See the section on handling partial `send()`s for a helper function to get around this.

Also, if the socket has been closed by either side, the process calling `send()` will get the signal `SIGPIPE`. (Unless `send()` was called with the `MSG_NOSIGNAL` flag.)

Example

```
1   int spatula_count = 3490;
2   char *secret_message = "The Cheese is in The Toaster";
3
4   int stream_socket, dgram_socket;
5   struct sockaddr_in dest;
6   int temp;
7
8   // first with TCP stream sockets:
9
10  // assume sockets are made and connected
11  //stream_socket = socket(...
12  //connect(stream_socket, ...
13
14  // convert to network byte order
15  temp = htonl(spatula_count);
16  // send data normally:
17  send(stream_socket, &temp, sizeof temp, 0);
18
19  // send secret message out of band:
20  send(stream_socket, secret_message, strlen(secret_message)+1, MSG_OOB);
21
22  // now with UDP datagram sockets:
23  //getaddrinfo(...
24  //dest = ... // assume "dest" holds the address of the destination
25  //dgram_socket = socket(...
26
27  // send secret message normally:
28  sendto(dgram_socket, secret_message, strlen(secret_message)+1, 0,
29          (struct sockaddr*)&dest, sizeof dest);
```

See Also

`recv()`, `recvfrom()`

shutdown()

Stop further sends and receives on a socket

Synopsis

```
#include <sys/socket.h>

int shutdown(int s, int how);
```

Description

That's it! I've had it! No more `send()`s are allowed on this socket, but I still want to `recv()` data on it! Or vice-versa! How can I do this?

When you `close()` a socket descriptor, it closes both sides of the socket for reading and writing, and frees the socket descriptor. If you just want to close one side or the other, you can use this `shutdown()` call.

As for parameters, `s` is obviously the socket you want to perform this action on, and what action that is can be specified with the `how` parameter. How can be `SHUT_RD` to prevent further `recv()`s, `SHUT_WR` to prohibit further `send()`s, or `SHUT_RDWR` to do both.

Note that `shutdown()` doesn't free up the socket descriptor, so you still have to eventually `close()` the socket even if it has been fully shut down.

This is a rarely used system call.

Return Value

Returns zero on success, or `-1` on error (and `errno` will be set accordingly).

Example

```
1   int s = socket(PF_INET, SOCK_STREAM, 0);
2
3   // ...do some send()s and stuff in here...
4
5   // and now that we're done, don't allow any more sends()s:
6   shutdown(s, SHUT_WR);
```

See Also

`close()`

`socket()`

Allocate a socket descriptor

Synopsis

```
#include <sys/types.h>
#include <sys/socket.h>

int socket(int domain, int type, int protocol);
```

Description

Returns a new socket descriptor that you can use to do sockety things with. This is generally the first call in the whopping process of writing a socket program, and you can use the result for subsequent calls to `listen()`, `bind()`, `accept()`, or a variety of other functions.

In usual usage, you get the values for these parameters from a call to `getaddrinfo()`, as shown in the example below. But you can fill them in by hand if you really want to.

Macro	Description
`domain`	`domain` describes what kind of socket you're interested in. This can, believe me, be a wide variety of things, but since this is a socket guide, it's going to be `PF_INET` for IPv4, and `PF_INET6` for IPv6.
`type`	Also, the `type` parameter can be a number of things, but you'll probably be setting it to either `SOCK_STREAM` for reliable TCP sockets (`send()`, `recv()`) or `SOCK_DGRAM` for unreliable fast UDP sockets (`sendto()`, `recvfrom()`). (Another interesting socket type is `SOCK_RAW` which can be used to construct packets by hand. It's pretty cool.)
`protocol`	Finally, the `protocol` parameter tells which protocol to use with a certain socket type. Like I've already said, for instance, `SOCK_STREAM` uses TCP. Fortunately for you, when using `SOCK_STREAM` or `SOCK_DGRAM`, you can just set the protocol to 0, and it'll use the proper protocol automatically. Otherwise, you can use `getprotobyname()` to look up the proper protocol number.

Return Value

The new socket descriptor to be used in subsequent calls, or `-1` on error (and `errno` will be set accordingly).

Example

```
 1  struct addrinfo hints, *res;
 2  int sockfd;
 3
 4  // first, load up address structs with getaddrinfo():
 5
 6  memset(&hints, 0, sizeof hints);
 7  hints.ai_family = AF_UNSPEC;      // AF_INET, AF_INET6, or AF_UNSPEC
 8  hints.ai_socktype = SOCK_STREAM; // SOCK_STREAM or SOCK_DGRAM
 9
10  getaddrinfo("www.example.com", "3490", &hints, &res);
11
12  // make a socket using the information gleaned from getaddrinfo():
13  sockfd = socket(res->ai_family, res->ai_socktype, res->ai_protocol);
```

See Also

accept( ), bind( ), getaddrinfo( ), listen( )

struct sockaddr and pals

Structures for handling internet addresses

Synopsis

```
#include <netinet/in.h>

// All pointers to socket address structures are often cast to pointers
// to this type before use in various functions and system calls:

struct sockaddr {
    unsigned short    sa_family;     // address family, AF_xxx
    char              sa_data[14];   // 14 bytes of protocol address
};


// IPv4 AF_INET sockets:

struct sockaddr_in {
    short             sin_family;    // e.g. AF_INET, AF_INET6
    unsigned short    sin_port;      // e.g. htons(3490)
    struct in_addr    sin_addr;      // see struct in_addr, below
    char              sin_zero[8];   // zero this if you want to
};

struct in_addr {
    unsigned long s_addr;            // load with inet_pton()
};


// IPv6 AF_INET6 sockets:

struct sockaddr_in6 {
    u_int16_t         sin6_family;   // address family, AF_INET6
    u_int16_t         sin6_port;     // port number, Network Byte Order
    u_int32_t         sin6_flowinfo; // IPv6 flow information
    struct in6_addr   sin6_addr;     // IPv6 address
    u_int32_t         sin6_scope_id; // Scope ID
};

struct in6_addr {
    unsigned char     s6_addr[16];   // load with inet_pton()
};
```

```
// General socket address holding structure, big enough to hold either
// struct sockaddr_in or struct sockaddr_in6 data:

struct sockaddr_storage {
    sa_family_t  ss_family;      // address family

    // all this is padding, implementation specific, ignore it:
    char        __ss_pad1[_SS_PAD1SIZE];
    int64_t     __ss_align;
    char        __ss_pad2[_SS_PAD2SIZE];
};
```

Description

These are the basic structures for all syscalls and functions that deal with internet addresses. Often you'll use getaddrinfo() to fill these structures out, and then will read them when you have to.

In memory, the struct sockaddr_in and struct sockaddr_in6 share the same beginning structure as struct sockaddr, and you can freely cast the pointer of one type to the other without any harm, except the possible end of the universe.

Just kidding on that end-of-the-universe thing…if the universe does end when you cast a struct sockaddr_in* to a struct sockaddr*, I promise you it's pure coincidence and you shouldn't even worry about it.

So, with that in mind, remember that whenever a function says it takes a struct sockaddr* you can cast your struct sockaddr_in*, struct sockaddr_in6*, or struct sockadd_storage* to that type with ease and safety.

struct sockaddr_in is the structure used with IPv4 addresses (e.g. "192.0.2.10"). It holds an address family (AF_INET), a port in sin_port, and an IPv4 address in sin_addr.

There's also this sin_zero field in struct sockaddr_in which some people claim must be set to zero. Other people don't claim anything about it (the Linux documentation doesn't even mention it at all), and setting it to zero doesn't seem to be actually necessary. So, if you feel like it, set it to zero using memset().

Now, that struct in_addr is a weird beast on different systems. Sometimes it's a crazy union with all kinds of #defines and other nonsense. But what you should do is only use the s_addr field in this structure, because many systems only implement that one.

struct sockadd_in6 and struct in6_addr are very similar, except they're used for IPv6.

struct `sockaddr_storage` is a struct you can pass to `accept()` or `recvfrom()` when you're trying to write IP version-agnostic code and you don't know if the new address is going to be IPv4 or IPv6. The `struct sockaddr_storage` structure is large enough to hold both types, unlike the original small `struct sockaddr`.

Example

```
1   // IPv4:
2
3   struct sockaddr_in ip4addr;
4   int s;
5
6   ip4addr.sin_family = AF_INET;
7   ip4addr.sin_port = htons(3490);
8   inet_pton(AF_INET, "10.0.0.1", &ip4addr.sin_addr);
9
10  s = socket(PF_INET, SOCK_STREAM, 0);
11  bind(s, (struct sockaddr*)&ip4addr, sizeof ip4addr);
```

```
1   // IPv6:
2
3   struct sockaddr_in6 ip6addr;
4   int s;
5
6   ip6addr.sin6_family = AF_INET6;
7   ip6addr.sin6_port = htons(4950);
8   inet_pton(AF_INET6, "2001:db8:8714:3a90::12", &ip6addr.sin6_addr);
9
10  s = socket(PF_INET6, SOCK_STREAM, 0);
11  bind(s, (struct sockaddr*)&ip6addr, sizeof ip6addr);
```

See Also

`accept()`, `bind()`, `connect()`, `inet_aton()`, `inet_ntoa()`

More References

You've come this far, and now you're screaming for more! Where else can you go to learn more about all this stuff?

Books

For old-school actual hold-it-in-your-hand pulp paper books, try some of the following excellent books. These redirect to affiliate links with a popular bookseller, giving me nice kickbacks. If you're merely feeling generous, you can paypal a donation to beej@beej.us. :-)

Unix Network Programming, volumes 1-2 by W. Richard Stevens. Published by Addison-Wesley Professional and Prentice Hall. ISBNs for volumes 1-2: 978-0131411555[49], 978-0130810816[50].

Internetworking with TCP/IP, volume I by Douglas E. Comer. Published by Pearson. ISBN 978-0136085300[51].

TCP/IP Illustrated, volumes 1-3 by W. Richard Stevens and Gary R. Wright. Published by Addison Wesley. ISBNs for volumes 1, 2, and 3 (and a 3-volume set): 978-0201633467[52], 978-0201633542[53], 978-0201634952[54], (978-0201776317[55]).

TCP/IP Network Administration by Craig Hunt. Published by O'Reilly & Associates, Inc. ISBN 978-0596002978[56].

Advanced Programming in the UNIX Environment by W. Richard Stevens. Published

---

[49] https://beej.us/guide/url/unixnet1
[50] https://beej.us/guide/url/unixnet2
[51] https://beej.us/guide/url/intertcp1
[52] https://beej.us/guide/url/tcpi1
[53] https://beej.us/guide/url/tcpi2
[54] https://beej.us/guide/url/tcpi3
[55] https://beej.us/guide/url/tcpi123
[56] https://beej.us/guide/url/tcpna

by Addison Wesley. ISBN 978-0321637734[57].

Web References

On the web:

BSD Sockets: A Quick And Dirty Primer[58] (Unix system programming info, too!)

The Unix Socket FAQ[59]

TCP/IP FAQ[60]

The Winsock FAQ[61]

And here are some relevant Wikipedia pages:

Berkeley Sockets[62]

Internet Protocol (IP)[63]

Transmission Control Protocol (TCP)[64]

User Datagram Protocol (UDP)[65]

Client-Server[66]

Serialization[67] (packing and unpacking data)

RFCs

RFCs[68]—the real dirt! These are documents that describe assigned numbers, programming APIs, and protocols that are used on the Internet. I've included links to a few of them here for your enjoyment, so grab a bucket of popcorn and put on your thinking cap:

RFC 1[69] —The First RFC; this gives you an idea of what the "Internet" was like just as it was coming to life, and an insight into how it was being designed from the ground up. (This RFC is completely obsolete, obviously!)

---

[57] https://beej.us/guide/url/advunix
[58] https://cis.temple.edu/~giorgio/old/cis307s96/readings/docs/sockets.html
[59] https://developerweb.net/?f=70
[60] http://www.faqs.org/faqs/internet/tcp-ip/tcp-ip-faq/part1/
[61] https://tangentsoft.net/wskfaq/
[62] https://en.wikipedia.org/wiki/Berkeley_sockets
[63] https://en.wikipedia.org/wiki/Internet_Protocol
[64] https://en.wikipedia.org/wiki/Transmission_Control_Protocol
[65] https://en.wikipedia.org/wiki/User_Datagram_Protocol
[66] https://en.wikipedia.org/wiki/Client-server
[67] https://en.wikipedia.org/wiki/Serialization
[68] https://www.rfc-editor.org/
[69] https://tools.ietf.org/html/rfc1

RFC 768[70] —The User Datagram Protocol (UDP)

RFC 791[71] —The Internet Protocol (IP)

RFC 793[72] —The Transmission Control Protocol (TCP)

RFC 854[73] —The Telnet Protocol

RFC 959[74] —File Transfer Protocol (FTP)

RFC 1350[75] —The Trivial File Transfer Protocol (TFTP)

RFC 1459[76] —Internet Relay Chat Protocol (IRC)

RFC 1918[77] —Address Allocation for Private Internets

RFC 2131[78] —Dynamic Host Configuration Protocol (DHCP)

RFC 2616[79] —Hypertext Transfer Protocol (HTTP)

RFC 2821[80] —Simple Mail Transfer Protocol (SMTP)

RFC 3330[81] —Special-Use IPv4 Addresses

RFC 3493[82] —Basic Socket Interface Extensions for IPv6

RFC 3542[83] —Advanced Sockets Application Program Interface (API) for IPv6

RFC 3849[84] —IPv6 Address Prefix Reserved for Documentation

RFC 3920[85] —Extensible Messaging and Presence Protocol (XMPP)

RFC 3977[86] —Network News Transfer Protocol (NNTP)

RFC 4193[87] —Unique Local IPv6 Unicast Addresses

---

[70] https://tools.ietf.org/html/rfc768
[71] https://tools.ietf.org/html/rfc791
[72] https://tools.ietf.org/html/rfc793
[73] https://tools.ietf.org/html/rfc854
[74] https://tools.ietf.org/html/rfc959
[75] https://tools.ietf.org/html/rfc1350
[76] https://tools.ietf.org/html/rfc1459
[77] https://tools.ietf.org/html/rfc1918
[78] https://tools.ietf.org/html/rfc2131
[79] https://tools.ietf.org/html/rfc2616
[80] https://tools.ietf.org/html/rfc2821
[81] https://tools.ietf.org/html/rfc3330
[82] https://tools.ietf.org/html/rfc3493
[83] https://tools.ietf.org/html/rfc3542
[84] https://tools.ietf.org/html/rfc3849
[85] https://tools.ietf.org/html/rfc3920
[86] https://tools.ietf.org/html/rfc3977
[87] https://tools.ietf.org/html/rfc4193

RFC 4506[88] —External Data Representation Standard (XDR)

The IETF has a nice online tool for searching and browsing RFCs[89].

---

[88]https://tools.ietf.org/html/rfc4506
[89]https://tools.ietf.org/rfc/

Index